D1593145

Tapestry of Grace

Tapestry of Grace

Untangling the Cultural Complexities
in Asian American Life and Ministry

Benjamin C. Shin

Sheryl Takagi Silzer

FOREWORD BY

John C. Kim

WIPF & STOCK · Eugene, Oregon

Wipf & Stock
An Imprint of Wipf and Stock Publishers
199 W. 8th Ave., Suite 3
Eugene, OR 97401

www.wipfandstock.com

PAPERBACK ISBN: 978-1-4982-3278-4
HARDCOVER ISBN: 978-1-4982-3280-7
EBOOK ISBN: 978-1-4982-3279-1

Manufactured in the U.S.A.

Foreword by Dr. John C. Kim
Figures 1–9 by Lauren Suhyun P. Yang
Figures 10–11 by Peter Silzer

To my wonderful, loving, and patient family: Jennifer, Adam, and Zachary Shin. I love you guys!

—Ben

To the Asian men and women whose culturally tangled lives have not fully experienced God's grace.

—Sheryl

Contents

CONTENTS

Section 3: Untangling Cultural Complexities and Weaving a Tapestry of Grace

Figures

Foreword

I'VE BEEN EAGERLY WAITING for a book like this. Drs. Benjamin Shin and Sheryl Takagi Silzer have done phenomenal work in unpacking the dynamics at work in Asian American ministries and providing practical, concrete solutions for Asian American churches to not just survive, but thrive. The strengths of this book are so many, from its comprehensive analysis and discussion on Asian American church models and the historical underpinnings of the Asian immigrant story of faith, to its insightful discussion on the multifaceted "clash of cultures" to which Asian American ministries in particular are susceptible. The book's remarkable ability to untangle the nuanced complexities of Asian American churches and offer applicable solutions to struggling immigrant ministries—coupled with on-point historical and scriptural references—reflects a deep commitment by the authors in "getting it right" and "making it practical," but "keeping it biblical."

The book's keen understanding of the cultural repercussions at work in Asian immigrant churches is a testament, in large part, to Dr. Shin's own personal story and passion in this context. I first met Dr. Shin in 1995 while he was the lead college pastor at a Korean American "duplex model" church. His ministry was flourishing but he was experiencing many of the generational and cultural conflicts that are referenced in this book. It was tough for him. At times, it was humiliating. And while these entanglements (and similar trials from the other "duplex model" churches in which he has served over the years) took various forms, what remained constant was Dr. Shin's humility, grace, patience, and forgiveness forged by the Gospel and his willingness to learn and appreciate the cultural influence of his first generation co-laborers (though he was born in America and every bit the Americanized Asian). Dr. Shin has harnessed these experiences into countless mentoring sessions with, and trainings of, Asian American seminarians,

FOREWORD

pastors, lay leaders, and college students contemplating full-time ministry. In this way and through this book, he is committed to ensuring that Asian American churches continue to play an unapologetically important role in the overall mosaic of America's evangelical and missional community. He has walked the talk.

Indeed, his love and care for the younger generations of Asian American Christian leaders and pastors as well as his respectful understanding of, and gratitude to, first-generation Asian Americans (like me) makes us kindred spirits. It explains why it has been an absolute joy to work with him—someone who is twenty-five years my junior—these past two decades in raising godly Asian American leaders and challenging Asian American churches to shed their bystander mentality and take spiritual ownership of America. Having lived for almost a half-century in America planting and serving in several Korean American immigrant churches as well as ministering and speaking to over a thousand such churches in America and around the world, this book blew me away in how it crystalized my own first-hand experiences and the patterns and symptoms that I have witnessed in many other Asian immigrant churches in both seasons of growth and seasons of difficulty.

It goes without saying that this book is a must-read to anyone serving in a predominantly Asian American Christian context. But I won't stop there. Like all matters in life, the ultimate answer for any immigrant church and their engagement of the culture within and without their walls—as this book refreshingly makes clear—is the inerrant Word of God. And in that regard, this book is not only for Asian Americans, but for any ethnic immigrant church in America seeking to establish their unique role in proclaiming the Gospel and furthering God's Kingdom in the States. Armed with the Bible and this book, you can't go wrong.

—John C. Kim, PhD
   Founder and President
   Global Leadership Development Institute (GLDI)

   Founder
   Jesus Awakening Movement for America (JAMA)

   Professor Emeritus
   California State University, Monterey Bay

xii

Preface

WE HAVE WRITTEN THIS book "Tapestry of Grace: Untangling the Cultural Complexities in Asian American Life and Ministry" to help both Asianized Americans (first-generation Asian language speakers) and Americanized Asians (second-generation and succeeding generation English speakers) to recognize the extent to which the misunderstandings they experience in life and ministry involve Asian and/or American cultural values. When both sides believe their way is the biblical rather than cultural way of doing things, there is no solution. We desire to describe the underlying cultural values that will enable the cultural complexities to be untangled in order for both groups to experience God's grace more fully.

Over fifteen years of teaching "The Asian Church in American Society" course at Talbot, we have seen how the students' lack of cultural self-knowledge (both Asian and American) has resulted in frustration, disappointment, bitterness, and anger from their inability to resolve these challenges in both their Asian life and their ministry in Asian American churches. Their lack of self-knowledge is a result of not understanding how the concepts of Confucian hierarchy, Buddhist reciprocity, and Taoist harmony have influenced their Asian cultural heritage and how their Asian values differ from American individualism as well as from biblical truth. This lack of understanding has fueled the "silent exodus" of Asian American young people from their immigrant churches, whether suddenly or in stages. Some of the stages of the exodus include the formation of different church models, the desire to start a church plant, and/or involvement in parachurch ministries. The similarity of Confucian values with some biblical values, particularly values in the Hebrew culture, easily leads to the misunderstanding that God's grace is based on fulfilling the social obligations of one's role in life and quietly following the wishes of authority figures, instead of being based on what God has done for us through the death of his Son on the cross for our sins. The need to earn God's favor by doing more may come from Confucian and Buddhist beliefs rather than from a heart that wants to serve and honor God. We believe that a greater understanding of Asian cultural values and the influence of Asian religious thinking (Confucianism, Buddhism, Taoism, etc.) will help both generations understand how their cultural values can be untangled from biblical truths so that Asian American Christians can experience God's grace more fully. Untangling the Asian and American values from the tapestry of grace will also create a desire to rebuild broken relationships between the generations caused by the clash of cultural values. By comparing Asian and American cultural practices with biblical truth, with God's help, all Asian American believers (first generation, second generation, and succeeding generations) can better understand what prevents them from experiencing God's grace and make the changes required to experience that amazing grace more fully.

—Benjamin C. Shin and Sheryl Takagi Silzer

Acknowledgments

I have so many people and groups to thank in helping this book come together. I want to thank my two churches, L.A. Hanmi and L.A. Open Door, for teaching me how to minister in an Asian American context. I want to thank KACF/CCM and AGO for my first exposure to Asian Americans. I appreciate all of the students that I've had the pleasure of learning from over the years at Talbot School of Theology. Special thanks goes to Lauren Suhyun P. Yang for her artistry in designing the graphics for my church models. Thanks also to my many mentors at Talbot School of Theology: Dennis Dirks, Mike Wilkins, Walt Russell, Mick Boersma, John Hutchison, Scott Rae, Clint Arnold, and Victor Rhee. Thanks also to my dad, John H. Shin, for always supporting me and encouraging me in my work. And last but not least, I thank my Lord Jesus Christ for saving me and calling me to His service!

—Ben

I also have many people to thank in helping this book to come together. First and foremost is my persevering and patient husband, who journeyed with me on the road to cultural self-discovery. Without his countless hours of editing, encouraging, and enabling, this book would not have become a reality. Second is my co-teacher, Ben Shin, who not only listened to my lectures over the years but also gave me numerous examples and insights from his own life and experiences. I'm also eternally grateful for the numerous family members and friends who have supported me over the years on my road to cultural self-discovery, as well as to the churches who invested in my life and ministry (Emmanuel Faith Community Church, Gardena

Valley Baptist, Portland Chinese Church, El Estero Presbyterian Church, Granada Heights Friends Church). In particular, I thank Keiko Yamamoto and the Nichigo ladies from El Estero Presbyterian Church, who graciously explained Japanese terms to me.

—Sheryl

Introduction

THE "TAPESTRY OF GRACE" seeks to untangle the Asian[1] and American[2] cultural complexities that hinder and prevent Asian American Christians from experiencing the grace of God in their lives and ministries. Asians and Americans are both created in God's image and, therefore, there are aspects of both cultures that can reflect the image of God. However, there are also aspects of both cultures that can distort what God intended and can prevent us from truly experiencing God's grace. When Christians view life from cultural perspectives, they often misinterpret their cultural values as being biblical values and thereby miss out on God's grace.

The inevitable clash of Asian and American cultures within the Asian American church can easily create an environment of suspicion, distrust, and anger between the first generation and the second and succeeding generations. Often neither side is aware of the cultural differences that contribute to these negative emotions. Because the differing cultural values impact every area of life, we (Ben and Sheryl) seek to enable both sides to understand the cultural clashes in order for both Asians and Americans to consider how God might want them to do things differently. That is, to make changes in order to more fully experience God's grace.

The actions of both the Asianized Americans (first-generation) and the Americanized Asians (second-generation and succeeding generations) demonstrate the lack of God's grace in their interactions with one another. The Americanized Asians are leaving the immigrant church. Some

1. For the purposes of this book, we will focus on only three Asian cultures: Chinese, Japanese, and Korean. These three groups share many philosophical and cultural similarities that are different from other Asian cultures.

2. In this book, we use the term "American" to refer to the generic U.S. American culture that values independence and individual choice.

are forming their own churches, others are finding ministry opportunities outside of the Asian context, and still others are leaving the church and Christianity altogether. Their stories of the frustration, shame, guilt, bitterness, and anger they experienced in their lives and ministries reveal the negative circumstances that caused them to leave. On the other hand, the Asianized Americans[3] are upset, angry, and bitter at their children and youth who are leaving the church and even leaving Christianity. Many of the first-generation believers have suffered in order to provide a better life for their children and they are shamed that the younger generation does not appreciate their efforts or understand their sacrifice. They also consider their children's actions to be unbiblical.

Many authors have recognized the lack of God's grace in Asian lives and ministry. Kang[4] states that aspects of both Asian and American culture need to be examined "in order to explore how a church's ministry will build on the foundation of grace."[5] Sugikawa and Wong cite Jao in listing several aspects of Asian culture, including "distant fathers, Confucian restraint, and internalized shame,"[6] and Lee defines Confucianism by hierarchy, patriarchy,[7] avoiding shame,[8] filial piety,[9] and gender issues.[10] These authors do not, however, explain how the Confucian ideals underlie Asian cultural practices or how they contribute to a cultural interpretation of biblical truth.

Park et al.[11] explain the need for Asian North American churches and pastors to be filled with grace, but they only briefly mention Asian cultural characteristics and do not explain how these cultural values inhibit grace. One major area that prevents people from experiencing God's grace is how authority is implemented by the older generation and how younger generations respond to Asian authoritarian practices. Asian authority is described

---

3. Asianized Americans are typically the first generation that live in the United States but prefer Asian rather than American values. Americanized Asians are typically second or succeeding generations that have adopted more American values than Asian cultural values.

4. Kang, "Conclusion," 202.

5. See Sugikawa and Wong, "Grace-Filled Households," 29.

6. Ibid., 23.

7. See Lee, "Healthy Leaders," 61.

8. Ibid., 65.

9. See Cha et al., "Multigenerational Households," 147.

10. See Cha and May, "Gender Relations," 166.

11. Park et al., Honoring the Generations, 3.

as being very paternalistic and comes from underlying Confucian values. Choong[12] describes these Confucian values as he shares his own experience with "extreme paternalistic authority" and how it influenced his own "paternalistic authoritarian leadership" in his ministry. Toyama[13] vividly describes the emotional upheaval of the lives and ministry of Asian American women caused by expectations, perfectionism, swallowing suffering, etc. which come from their primary domestic role. The book *More than Serving Tea* seeks to change this view of Asian women. The lack of validation for Asian women in leadership positions pushes Asian women to look for ministry opportunities in non-Asian churches or in parachurch organizations. Russell Jeung[14] states that the Asian authoritarian leadership has also taught the younger generation that they have to earn acceptance. As a result, neither generation understands that God's grace does not have to be earned.

Another group of authors recognizes similarities between Confucian and Christian ideals and discusses their compatibility. Fenggang Yang[15] reports that Chinese evangelical Christians claim they can "remain truthful to both Christianity and Confucianism without being syncretic." Yoo and Chung[16] describe Korean American Christianity as weaving Confucian values such as in "filial piety, respect for parents, family centeredness, and work ethic" with Christian values. Although Tokunaga[17] recognizes aspects of Confucianism that are similar to Christianity, he believes these aspects clash with Christianity, particularly in regard to the treatment of women. On the other hand, even some non-Asians believe that they can learn about Christianity from Confucian concepts.[18]

Although these cultural problems involving filial piety, respect for parents, family centeredness, and work ethic are readily identified in Asian lives and ministry, they are seldom discussed in relation to helping Asian Christians discover that their cultural practices stem from Confucian, Buddhist, and Taoist roots. There is little discussion about how these cultural roots prevent Asian Americans from experiencing God's grace or about

12. Choong, *Counter-Cultural Paradigmatic Leadership*, 3.
13. Toyama, "Perfectionistic Tendencies," 50-68.
14. Jeung, *Faithful Generations*, 72–73.
15. Yang, *Chinese Christians*, 154.
16. Yoo and Chung, *Religion and Spirituality*, 164–65.
17. Tokunaga, *Invitation to Lead*, 37–38.
18. Ten Elshoff, *Confucius for Christians*, 4.

what Asian American Christians can do about the situation. This book seeks to help Asian American Christians discover how their cultural heritage impacts their lives and ministry, how they can examine their cultural beliefs in light of Scripture, and what they can do to reconnect with and live in the grace God freely offers. We desire the grace of God to flourish in Asian American lives and ministry so as to build up the Kingdom of God.

This book is divided into three sections. Section 1 is written by Ben and describes various aspects of the present day Asian American churches as they have sought to address the cultural complexities they face and how these complexities relate to biblical truths. Section 2 is written by Sheryl to untangle the cultural complexities of the Asian and American cultural influences in Asian American life and ministry, particularly influences from Confucianism, Buddhism, and Taoism. In section 3 both Ben and Sheryl share their personal journeys about untangling their Asian American cultural backgrounds that helped them to experience God's grace more fully. Ben concludes with ideas about how the lessons in this book can impact the Asian American church if the cultural complexities are untangled so that both communities—Asianized Americans and Americanized Asians—can experience God's grace and that God's Kingdom can be clearly seen in the Asian American church.

SECTION 1

The Tangled Cultural Complexities in the Asian American Church

IN THIS BOOK WE are seeking to close the generation gap between the more traditional immigrant Asian church and succeeding generations of Asian American Christians in order for both groups to experience God's grace. We hope and pray that better understanding and cooperation will result in reversing the trend of the "silent exodus"[19] that has been affecting Asian and Asian American churches significantly for the last thirty years. This section will deal with a number of important questions facing the Asian American church today: Why does the first-generation Asian church do what they do? Why is relationship so important for Asians, especially within the family and the church? Why is there so much conflict between the two generations? Many of the answers to these and other questions lie within a greater understanding of Asian culture.

Our hope and prayer for you is that you will see the "other side" of these issues and have a greater understanding of and even an appreciation for a people and culture that is different from yours. Again, the issue here is not a difference necessarily between right and wrong but simply of differences in style and culture. Many of these issues are not a moral issue, but rather a cultural one. Ephesians 4:3 sums up our goal together for the church, no matter what side or generation you are a part of. Paul encourages believers to be "eager to maintain the unity of the Spirit in the bond of peace." May this be the prayer for yourself and your church to the glory of God.

19. Lee, "Silent Exodus," 50–54 and "Silent No More," 38–47.

In chapter 1 Ben describes the different church models that Asian Americans have developed to address the growing chasm between the first generation and succeeding generations mainly based on language difference (Asian versus English language). Chapter 2 reveals how the concept of shame in Asian cultures has impacted social interaction and how it compares not only with the biblical concept of shame but also with the life of the first-century Christians. Chapter 3 describes how the concept of grace of the first-century church is similar to some aspects of Asian culture, being built on reciprocity, in contrast to a more Western unilateral concept of grace. A comparison of Asian reciprocity with biblical grace further clarifies what our relationship with God should look like. In chapter 4 Ben explains a major struggle of the second-generation church leaders: that is, should they stay in the immigrant church or should they plant a church? In chapter 5 Ben describes how spirituality is shaped and influenced by Asian cultural values. He compares some of the similarities and differences between Korean and Chinese spirituality.

1

Got Church?

Introduction

OVER THE YEARS, ASIAN Americans have chosen to attend a number of new types of churches which have emerged in the U.S. No longer is it as simple as just finding an Asian immigrant church somewhere in a city. Rather, many different models of church are now frequented by Asian American Christians all throughout the U.S. This chapter gives an overview of these different church models, describes some of their strengths and challenges, and offers insights into why different models are preferred over others. Credit must be given to Dr. Hoover Wong, who originally came up with a number of church models[1] in the chapter called "Church Models for Mission" in his book *Coming Together or Coming Apart?*[2] I (Ben) have updated, changed, and added other church models to his work in light of more recent developments.

The Biblical Basis for Church

So what is the biblical basis for the local church in the Scriptures? Surprisingly, the nature of the church in the Bible is more universal than localized. While many new models and kinds of churches have arisen over the years, including the seeker-sensitive church, the emergent church, the house church, and the megachurch, the term *ekklesia* in the New Testament is more often referred to in its universal scope rather than in its local use. Dr. Robert Saucy, in his book *The Church in God's Program,* writes that, "the concept of a physical assembly gives way to the spiritual unity of all

1. I use four of Wong's models: Room-to-Let, Duplex, Townhouse, Hotel.
2. Wong, *Coming Together,* 198–215.

believers in Christ. *Ekklesia* is this sense is not the assembly itself but rather those constituting it; they are the church whether actually assembled or not."[3] He points to the universal church throughout the New Testament in such passages as Matt 16:18; Acts 8:3, 9:31; 1 Cor 12:28, 15:9; Eph 1:22–23; and Col 1:18. While the universality of the church is strongly supported in the Scripture, Millard Erickson adds another dimension concerning the local church in his book on systematic theology: ". . . while it is universal in nature, it finds expression in local groupings of believers which display the same qualities as does the body of Christ as a whole."[4]

The central question then to this whole issue should not be "should I go to church or not, but rather which kind of church should I be a part of as a congregation member?" The choices are numerous and probably still increasing in the future. This next section will highlight the nine different types of church models that Asian Americans have been attending, serving in, and being a part of over the years.

Nine Church Models Asian Americans Attend

The following nine church models represent a variety of approaches which are being used within the Asian American Christian setting. Each model includes positive and negative aspects that must be considered.

1) The Room-for-Let Model

The Room-for-Let[5] designation was termed by Dr. Hoover Wong to describe a small segment or room within an immigrant church which was devoted to English-speaking church members. These members could be part of a youth group or a college group led by an English-speaking second-generation pastor or sometimes even by an outsourced Caucasian pastor based on his English language proficiency. This model is by far the most common model found across America for Asian Americans.

---

3. Saucy, *The Church*, 16–17.

4. Erickson, *Christian Theology*, 1034.

5. Wong, *Coming Together*, 203. Wong's term is "Room-to-Let."

ROOM FOR LET MODEL

The need for the Room-for-Let model of church arose when the children of the parents in an immigrant church needed a place to worship in English because they could not understand or relate to the main service that is often conducted in the Asian language spoken by the first-generation church members. For this reason, the Room-for-Let model is used to keep the children in the church so as to prevent them from leaving to go to another church. Wong writes, "This is the boarding-house approach, as space is set aside for those who are alien to the root culture and language. It is a holding action concerning the youth. Defection is delayed."[6]

While the Room-for-Let model may seem like a good immediate solution for the church and its need, it is at best only a short-term solution. Eventually, the children will get older and, if they stay in the church, will get married and have their own families. Typically, families will want to be with other families. Peers of the same life stage enjoy being with each other. Thus, the small Room-for-Let will not be sufficient to meet the different needs of the family members when different ages and stages of family emerge. At that point, greater attention and resources need to be provided for the English speakers or else they may look for another church that could better accommodate the needs of their families.

The strength of the Room-for-Let model is only a short-term advantage. It keeps the family unit together at the same church site temporarily,

6. Ibid., 203.

and generations can be more intimate because people from different generations will know each other well. This model will have a strong family feel to it. But at the same time, due to the normally small size of a congregation, everyone in the church needs to serve. A lack of resources is often a huge issue in the Room-for-Let model. Because the congregation is typically small, the same workers serve for a very long time. This can often lead to fatigue and sometimes even burnout. Another issue is that many of these workers are not fed spiritually and feel the strain of serving without the benefit of personal growth. These are but a few of the many plights that small church congregations face.

2) The Duplex Model

This next model, the Duplex,[7] is an upgrade from the Room to Let model. It is often the result of the members from the Room-for-Let model just getting older, more mature, more numerous, and financially stronger. The basic structure of the Duplex model is two different congregations: an English-speaking one and an immigrant church that speaks the mother tongue. The two groups co-exist next to each other, but are under one leadership. If the denomination is Presbyterian, both congregations would be under the elders, for example. Or, if the church is part of a Baptist denomination, then both congregations would be under a board of deacons. Either way, every decision, especially of budgetary nature, goes through the leadership of the first-generation immigrant church.

7. Ibid., 203.

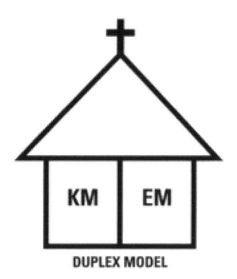

DUPLEX MODEL

The advantages of the Duplex model are numerous. One of the biggest advantages for the Duplex model is that it again keeps the English speakers (English Ministry or EM) and the immigrant first-generation members (Korean Ministry or KM) on the same campus. For a culture that strongly values a collectivist community, this model allows for the maintenance of this practice. This model is favorable to the English side because it provides many resources such as facilities, water and power, copy machines, internet service, office space, etc. These resources are often taken for granted, especially because the first-generation church typically pays for and provides these services for the English-speaking church without cost. These provisions are often not appreciated until the English-speaking church has to start sharing in the payment for these resources or, in some cases, leaves and starts their own church and needs to start paying for everything themselves.

Another very big strength of the Duplex model is that it gives the opportunity for the older members of the immigrant church to see their children and grandchildren on a weekly basis. This may seem strange to a second-generation Asian American, especially since the two congregations worship at separate times and locations. But again, because the collectivist mindset of Asians is a strong dynamic within the culture, to know that fellow family members are on the same church site or campus is very assuring. For example, in many Korean churches, lunch is served after the service, and people from different generations gather inside a fellowship hall or banquet room. Family members may run into each other by just passing through the line and be able to say "hello" to each other. Even though this contact would be brief, it would be regular and frequent enough for the older generation to be pleased. For this reason, many first-generation immigrants would prefer the Duplex model.

One of the disadvantages of the Duplex model is the lack of training and empowerment for future generations. This includes everything from financial matters to paying bills to making decisions about the future direction of the church. Because the first generation typically makes all of the decisions without consulting the second-generation leadership, there is limited opportunity for the younger people to learn and, in some cases, even to fail. This practice results in a largely missed opportunity for growth and development. Experience in leadership is vital because sometimes the younger second generation has little to no idea what to do because the older generation has done everything for them. With this unhealthy reliance on the first-generation leaders comes a lack of preparation to be responsible and ready to make decisions concerning finances, church matters, property decisions, etc. This lack of experience shows up over time when the second generation is given the opportunity to lead without having enough experience or training.

3) The Triplex Model

The Triplex model of church is a unique model to the Chinese church, which is typically comprised of three congregations: Mandarin-speaking, Cantonese-speaking, and English-speaking. The dynamics for this model are very sensitive and tricky at the same time. Whereas, the Duplex model has two different congregations to work with, the Triplex model adds yet another congregation to the mix.

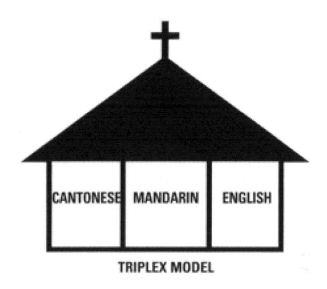

TRIPLEX MODEL

Perhaps the biggest struggle with the Triplex model is the potential power struggles that can occur between the three congregations. Below are some of the challenges that emerge from this church model. First comes the issue of representation of the leadership. When the leadership board is formed, the process by which the board members are chosen may be based on the size of each respective congregation. For example, if the Mandarin-speaking congregation is the largest within the Triplex model, then they will have the most leaders on the board to represent their interests. While this makes sense at one level, another challenge is to have adequate representation from the other congregations, especially from the English-speaking congregation. The leaders from the other congregations may overpower the voices from the English-speaking congregation. Adding to this, if the English-speaking board member is younger, then within the Confucian hierarchical mindset of the other leaders, his voice could be ignored and the needs of the younger generation could go unrecognized.

The challenge within the Triplex model is not just based on the size of each group but also based on which congregation is the oldest or the first group to be a part of the church. Sometimes, the original or founding group may feel entitled to be able to have the most influence because they were part of the original founding group. This may also mean that they may be the oldest members by age within the church. Again, due to the hierarchical nature of Confucian thought in Asian cultures, the older members of the congregation may feel that they have the most authority within the church and thus should be the only ones to make the majority of the decisions for the church as a whole. This can be a very challenging scenario to work through.

The only way for the Triplex model to work well is for the leaders of each of the three congregations to respect and defer to each other well enough for the other to succeed. Two of the best Triplex models are Bread of Life in Lomita, California and Boston Chinese Evangelical Church in Boston, Massachusetts. These are long-standing churches that have worked together well for many years even with many leadership changes. Humility, more than anything, marks the leaders of each congregation and thus the members follow their example, leading to peace and harmony in these churches.

4) The Townhouse Model

For many in the Asian American church, the Townhouse model[8] seems like the dream model of church. Much like young homeowners buying a new townhouse, there is much excitement generated by the thought of having something that they personally own. This is the biggest draw of the Townhouse model of church. The English congregation is able to have their own leadership separate from the immigrant church and are thus able to determine their own vision, theology, budget, and programs.

8. Wong, *Coming Together*, 205.

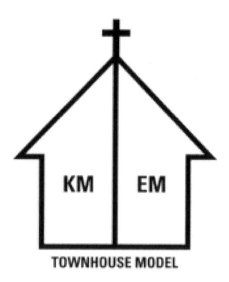

TOWNHOUSE MODEL

The main characteristic of the Townhouse model of church is that it has the ability to sustain its own leadership, budget, and, sometimes, facilities. This model often emerges and develops from a Duplex model. Whereas the Duplex model is under the leadership of an immigrant church, the Townhouse model is the result of a congregation that has matured over time, growing older in age, larger in the number of members, and stronger in financial giving. This allows for an autonomy in which the English side is seen now as "grownups" in the church. One of the main traits of this model is that it typically takes a long time to develop. It also requires leaders on both the immigrant side and the English side to stay together in partnership as a church. This may even result in being on the same church campus but using different buildings or segments of the site.

One of the first things that stands out for the Townhouse model is that the nonimmigrant church often will take on a different name from the mother church. In some cases, it will be a variation from the name of the mother church, but in other cases, it will be quite different. In Los Angeles, California, the Young Nak Celebration Church (YNCC) is the oldest and most developed Townhouse model for any English-speaking Korean church. With a history of twenty-five years, it has spent half of the time as a Duplex church model and the other half as a Townhouse model. YNCC is across the street from its mother church, Young Nak Presbyterian Church. The two churches work together in partnership, even though they have separate leadership boards that, for the most part, make separate decisions autonomously from each other.

Despite the independence of the two congregations, there are many areas in which the two churches still share together in partnership. For example, YNCC assists the Korean church financially by paying rent to help pay for the mortgage as well as a significant amount to aid the education department of the church. The Korean side of the church takes care of the education department all the way from kindergarten up to college-age students. People who graduate from college then move into YNCC and thus are considered a part of the English ministry. While this scenario may seem ideal in many ways, it has also led to some hardships as well, including the whole issue of quality control between the two congregations and their respective views of Christian education. This issue will manifest itself in discussions on topics such as which language is preferred (English or Korean); the theological perspective taught (Presbyterian, Baptist, Covenantal, Dispensational); the style and content of the pedagogy (morality versus Bible content); and even the issue of the hiring and qualifications of the staff and pastors.

One of the strongest advantages of the Townhouse model is that it allows for autonomy and development for the leadership in their decision-making. It also allows members of the congregation to mature as they serve and take greater ownership of the church. No longer are these members under the care and tutelage of their parents' church where everything was previously provided for (e.g., the facilities, power and water, mortgage, copy machines, custodial service, and much more). This independence now causes the members of the English ministry to grow up and step up since there is no longer anyone else to provide for everything. This change may be difficult at first because there may not have been much intentional mentorship from the first generation. Nevertheless, the second generation typically learns quickly, oftentimes through trial and error.

The success of the Townhouse model of church is really dependent on four areas: 1) the willingness of the leaders from both congregations to work together; 2) the ability to communicate clearly and frequently between the two congregations; 3) tenacity and patience by both congregations and the ability to forgive the other; 4) congregations that are willing to be cross-cultural and cross-generational.

The Townhouse model of church works well when the leaders from both the immigrant church and the English-speaking church are willing to work together in partnership. This requires patience, humility, understanding, and a level of cultural sensitivity to the other group. When this is modeled well, especially from the lead pastors of each congregation, then the rest of the leadership and eventually the congregation will be empowered to follow suit. If, however, the leaders from both churches are quarreling, speaking against the other leaders, or gossiping about other leaders, then it is only a matter of time before the relationship and even the churches will collide, have conflict, and possibly even separate. The relationship between the two lead pastors of the congregations here is the most important factor that will keep the Townhouse model intact.

Another important factor that will aid in the success of the Townhouse model is clear and frequent communication. Obviously, this is an essential principle for any organization or relationship. Without it, there will certainly be misunderstandings and ultimately even conflicts. One example of the need for communication is the use of group facilities. For example, there may be occasions when the sanctuary may be double-booked by two different groups for the same time slot. Without a centralized place to confirm the booking (e.g., a meeting, a memo, or an e-mail posted publicly), problems could arise. Sometimes two large groups are expecting to use the same facility, not knowing that the other had already booked it. The double booking comes as a surprise to the other group, and then difficult conversations must take place. But with clear and frequent communication, in many forms, such conflicts can be avoided.

Just as in any relationship, tenacity, patience, and even forgiveness are key components for the Townhouse model of church. There will be times when one congregation or the other violates a use of a facility, of resources, or of a time spot displacing the other group and even potentially offending them. Just as in a human family, there may be times of hurt, conflict, and misunderstandings between the two churches. For the believer, the importance of forgiveness "just as God in Christ Jesus has forgiven us" (Eph 4:32) is vital in order to keep the churches on good terms. Again, without this essential and fundamental Christian virtue, the future of the Townhouse model churches would be doomed.

The final necessary conditions for the Townhouse model to flourish are flexible and understanding congregations from both churches who understand and even embrace cross-cultural and cross-generational values. This sense of "family" can extend significantly in a Townhouse model because even though the English congregation is separate from the immigrant church, in many cases, the immigrant church is either across the street or just a building away. In other words, congregation members of the English-speaking side feel that the immigrant side is far away enough but at the same time close enough to maintain relationships while respectfully keeping a healthy distance. This seems like the ideal circumstance for many older Asian Americans.

5) The Hotel Model

A recent growing trend for many Asian Americans is the movement out of Asian American churches and into large Caucasian churches. This is an example of the Hotel model.[9] This trend has occurred on two levels: 1) with the congregants and 2) with the pastoral staff. This section will explore the different causes of this recent trend. There are a number of reasons that the Hotel model draws Asian Americans.

HOTEL MODEL

Younger congregants such as Millennials may be drawn to Hotel model churches because these churches often have a diverse mixture of people from many different ethnicities and cultures. The draw to diversity certainly has biblical precedent as seen in passages such as Rev 5:9; 7:9 where the future eschatological glimpse of heaven will be a cross-cultural choir

9. Wong, *Coming Together*, 206.

of people from every tongue, tribe, language, and nation singing a chorus of "Worthy is the Lamb!" While this picture seems very attractive initially, it is also very challenging to establish long-term relational depth and community.

Part of the challenge of the Hotel model is that while Asian Americans enjoy the resources and the lack of emphasis on culture, neither the majority culture of the church nor the Asian Americans know how to relate well to each other. Awkward questions from well-meaning Caucasians such as "Where are you from?" seek to discover what the person's mother country and ethnicity may be. I was born in Pasadena, California and grew up in a Caucasian church, but I was often asked, "Where are you from?" My honest answer was Pasadena!

One of the biggest reasons that many young Asian Americans have fled to these large churches is to escape from the cultural difficulties in their previous church and to renew themselves spiritually. They may be escaping some of the heavy responsibilities and duties that they held in leadership positions in their previous church. In many cases, these people need some time to recover from their fatigue in serving the church ever since they were young. They may also be escaping some of the cultural hardships that may have troubled them, and in some cases have caused great tension and even conflict.

At the same time, these large megachurches can bring much comfort and encouragement during these interim times of sabbatical. Many of these churches have excellent preachers and dynamic worship teams that make the church service experience exhilarating and inspiring for the tired, burned out leader. This kind of church experience is often exactly what is needed for wounded workers during a time of recovery. With no responsibilities to fulfill, people can participate at the audience level without any other concerns or distractions. They can rest and recover. In addition, large megachurches have tremendous resources and specific ministries that could cater to the needs of burned out leaders.

Another benefit of being in the Hotel model is that there can be greater anonymity. A person can come and go without being noticed. There are no responsibilities or duties to perform. A person who is exhausted and burned out spiritually has no desire to serve at this time or to give anything, for that matter. He just wants to receive as much as he can without cost. This response is certainly understandable, since many of these people gave above and beyond the call of duty in their earlier ministry, possibly for many years!

6) The Church Plant Model

For many Asian American pastors, the Church Plant has been the most attractive and sought after model among all the different church models. Some of these church plants started from scratch, but a number of them came out of English ministries that left an immigrant church after much conflict. Some of the reasons for a church plant include: 1) the desire to become multiethnic; 2) differing theological or vision perspectives; 3) too many conflicts and disputes; 4) firing/termination of the English Ministry pastor.

CHURCH PLANT MODEL

One of the biggest reasons that church plants originate out of Asian immigrant churches is the desire to become multiethnic. The most common reason for the church plant stems from a visionary English-speaking pastor who feels called to reach the community and to diversify the congregation. Oftentimes, an Asian immigrant church may be located in a predominately Hispanic area, for example. Despite the church's location and his longing to reach out to the local community, the English-speaking pastor may feel restricted from inviting the "neighbors" because of the church's many Asian cultural traits—ranging from the name of the church to the distinct Asian smells of the foods served at the church. These factors may become a deterrent to non-Asians attending the church. For this reason, it seems logical to break away from the immigrant church, establish a new church with a more non-Asian name, and then begin reaching out to people other than Asian Americans.

While becoming a multiethnic church may seem practical, exciting, and even biblical (see Rev 5:9; 7:9) most Asian Americans in the church are probably not ready nor equipped to plant a multicultural church. Here are a few thoughts as well as reasons why the typical Asian American Christian may not be ready to plant a church. First of all, starting a church plant is very difficult due to financial issues, location challenges, and the requirement for the starting group to take ownership in doing just about everything since they are the only people available. One of the biggest warning signs to be aware of in starting a church plant is the state of mind of the initial starting group. If, for example, the church plant begins under unfortunate circumstances (i.e., a church split, firing, conflict, etc.), the members coming out to the church plant may be hurt, embittered, or even jaded. It is certainly not ideal to start a church plant with such people as the pioneer group. It is best to start a church plant based on a positive leading and calling of the Lord in order to reach a specific community or group of people. An untimely beginning of a church plant filled with disgruntled people will often lead to the new church plant splitting again in the future.

There are, however, a number of wonderful reasons to begin a church plant. These include the following: 1) a unique vision to reach a specific group or kind of people; 2) a need in an area where there is no Asian American church; 3) a healthy send-off from a church due to size and logistical circumstances. Many times, a church planting pastor is very visionary and ambitious in his desire to reach people such as the unchurched or the marginalized. An example of this is New Song Community Church in Santa Ana, where the church's tagline is to reach the "misfits." What this means is that they invite unchurched people who would not typically walk into a traditional church. The music for the service is contemporary, possibly even secular, in order to set up a seeker-friendly environment for them to feel comfortable. New Song has successfully reached many marginalized people over the years who would never be stereotyped as a "church goer."

7) The Independent Church Model

The Independent Church model is very similar to the Church Plant model. The Independent church may have even existed previously as a church plant. The main differences are the following: 1) size and fiscal strength; 2) ownership of property; and 3) ability to plant other churches.

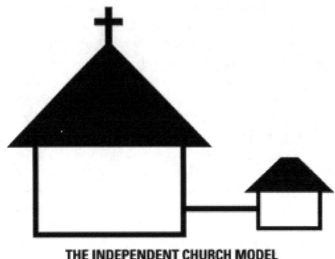

THE INDEPENDENT CHURCH MODEL

The first characteristic that marks the Independent model is that it may be much bigger than a typical church plant. It may range from 300 to 500 attendees or members and may include different life stages and ages. Whereas a church plant may begin with only college students or young single adults, an independent church will have older, established adults, married couples, youth, and children, in addition to college and single adults. With this new range of members also comes greater financial stability as well as support that allows a pastor and even staff to be paid a consistent full-time salary. The independent church is not dependent on a denomination or association, but is able to sustain itself comfortably.

This leads to the second trait of an independent church in that, due to the increased number of members as well as financial strength, they are now able to purchase their own property. This is a more recent trend that has been increasing in only the last ten to fifteen years. The typical church plant is reliant on different venues to rent including schools, hotels, community centers, and even other older and declining churches. This kind of rental situation has posed many hardships and challenges, including setting up and tearing down everything from the stage, sound equipment, lighting, signs, the nursery, etc. for the church activities. Often, all of this equipment is stored in trailers or rental trucks and must be brought in early on Sunday morning by a dedicated staff of volunteers. Owning property solves this cumbersome task since storage, security, and other factors are already taken care of because the church owns the property.

While this kind of model seems ideal and wonderful, it often comes with a high cost at every level. The challenge of finding a suitable property is only the beginning. Getting all the proper permits and papers for meeting is yet another challenge. Zoning for parking and heavy traffic create further challenges for the Independent church. Constructing a new building or even renovating an old office building into a church with theater seating and a stage takes lots of time, money, and creativity. These are but a few challenges that independent churches face.

Over the last fifteen years, a few independent churches have emerged in various cities in Southern California. One of the first such independent churches in the Asian American community is a church called The Garden Church in Chatsworth in the San Fernando Valley area. This church started as a small college church situated near the campus of UCLA. At the time, the church started it was known as Westside Oikos Church. The church was a part of a network of two other churches in Southern California. Thus, the majority of the attendees during the early days were all college students from the nearby university. Over the years, the church grew steadily, and the former college students graduated, began full-time jobs, and started giving substantially to the church. The church decided to relocate to the San Fernando Valley and was able to buy its own property. The church flourished with many young parents with small children who came to the church due to a strong children's Sunday School program. The church continues to grow to this day.

Another Independent Church model is the Church of the Southland located in Placentia, California. This church began as a Duplex church as the English Ministry of a large Korean church in Orange County. The English-speaking group decided to break off from the mother church and started a church plant meeting at a local health club for a few years. They were able to purchase a medium-sized property in the 1990s, and the church grew bigger, again due to a strong children's Sunday School program. They recently purchased property and built a church on a much larger piece of land in Placentia, California, and are experiencing exponential growth.

Two more independent churches in Southern California are Living Hope Community Church in Brea, California and Berean Community

Church in Irvine, California. Both were able to secure their property in cities that have a high population of Asian Americans and were able to buy pre-existing buildings that they needed to convert into more suitable worship sanctuaries. Both of these churches grew fairly rapidly. One of the contributing factors to the rapid growth of Berean Community Church was the presence of a local university, UC Irvine, and a campus parachurch ministry called Crossroads Campus Ministries that encouraged its members to attend Berean. Berean was very supportive and reciprocated the favor by providing speakers and even financial support for the campus fellowship. This partnership has successfully lasted for more than twelve years, and both groups continue to flourish.

One final trait of the Independent Church model is its ability to then send people out and establish a new church plant as well. The best example of this is Berean Community Church that sent one of its pastors to Northern California to plant Berean Mission Church. Not only did the pastor go, but so did a number of the members of the church in Irvine to help support and establish the new church plant. This new church is rapidly growing now in the Bay Area.

Another example of an independent church that has planted four new church plants is Lighthouse Bible Church in San Diego, California. This church started out as a church plant nearly eighteen years ago and has planted three other Lighthouse Churches: one in Orange County, one in the Bay Area, and one in Glendale, California. The original church has not only planted three church plants, the churches now work together as an alliance as part of the Lighthouse Bible Church network.

8) The Satellite/Multisite Model

Another model of church that has recently been utilized by Asian Americans is known as the Satellite model or Multisite church. While this model has been used for years by the larger Caucasian megachurches around America (i.e., Willow Creek Community Church, Saddleback Church, etc.), it has only been explored by Asian American churches in America in the last ten to fifteen years. The structure of a Satellite/Multisite model of church is that there is a mother church or main campus that works together with other sites or sister campuses within their network of churches. There are two main ways that these churches have worked: one is by sharing campus pastors who may speak at the different sites but present the same message or, more recently, the use of a prerecorded video or simulcast of the main or lead pastor preaching simultaneously to all of the different sites.

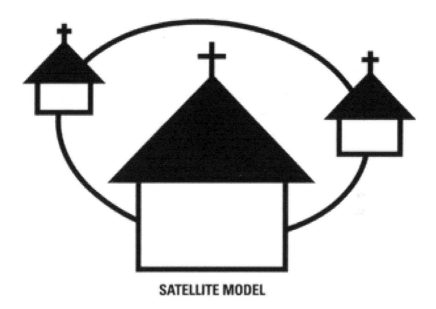

SATELLITE MODEL

The first type of Satellite/Multisite model of church is used by New Song Community Church in Santa Ana, California, a well-known example of this model. Initially, there were three campuses: the mother campus in Irvine, the Los Angeles campus in Culver City, and the Northern Orange County (NOC) campus in Brea. The pastoral staff from all three campuses would meet during the week to plan and prepare for the same series and message that would be delivered the following Sunday by each campus pastor respectively. While the message was the same in content, pastors from the different campuses would add their own specific style to their message. This model works well for many reasons but also brings challenges. The model requires many coordinating meetings among the pastors. Coordination may be challenging because each pastor may have his own understanding or interpretation of the selected passage. Coordination may restrict the freedom of the pastors who follow the designated plan each week. New Song has since abandoned this approach to their preaching.

Another example of this model is Young Nak Celebration Church (YNCC) and its Jefferson Campus that follows a structure similar to New Song Church.

The more common practice for the Satellite/Multisite model of church of today is to have a prerecorded video of the senior pastor who gives the sermon while a live campus pastor is present at each site to greet people and to bring the relational element of church to the members. This practice is very common with large megachurches who have a well-known senior pastor. One of the best examples of this is Pastor Rick Warren at Saddleback Church in Southern California. Within the Saddleback network of churches several remote sites watch Pastor Warren preach the sermon. It is interesting to note that many of these sites have a high percentage of Asian Americans in attendance, sometimes ranging as high as 60 percent of the congregation. While traditional Asian Americans do not prefer the video format of message due to its impersonal nature, many young Asian Americans are starting to flock to these kinds of churches. Part of the attraction to the Multisite model may be due to the similar reasons that young Asian Americans choose the Hotel model of church: i.e., the desire to be inconspicuous and to be away from the Asian church for renewal and refreshment from some of the cultural challenges that have hurt them in the past.

It will be interesting to see if Asian Americans continue to be a part of this model of church for the long term or not. My prediction is that they will not be part of it for the long term because they will miss the interaction, fellowship, and relationships that the other church models offer. Group interaction can be sustained, however, if Asian Americans find and plug into good small groups in order to experience community. Participation in small groups could sustain them to be a part of a multisite church for the long haul.

9) The 2-in-1 Model

The most recent church model, the 2-in-1 model, has been prevalent among Korean churches, especially in Southern California. The basic structure of this model is two congregations that are led by one pastor. The one pastor is usually a younger pastor who is bilingual and able to speak both the mother tongue and English; thus being able to preach to both congregations. Davis Korean Church in Northern California is an example of this model. This church has produced at least three pastors (Jim-bob Park, Daniel Kim, and David Yi) who led both congregations in Davis and then went on to lead much larger churches around California. Jim-bob Park leads Oriental Mission Church and Family Chapel. Daniel Kim led Sarang Community Church and Holy Wave; and David Yi leads New Vision Church in Milpitas. The one outstanding trait shared by all these men is that they are all able to preach very well in Korean and in English. They were also fairly young when they became the senior pastor and, thus, were able to lead both congregations. This model has been seen as the best model to lead a Duplex or Townhouse church because there is only one pastor overseeing both. This model eliminates communication problems and differing visions. From an optimistic point of view, this model seems very promising. A more pessimistic evaluation, though, considers that this model can also be seen as a controlling, hierarchical model that is imperialistic in nature.

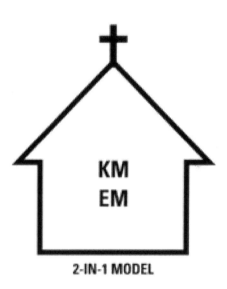

2-IN-1 MODEL

There are a number of other concerns for this 2-in-1 model. First, the model can easily overwork the lone pastor who leads both congregations. Essentially, this pastor is watching over two churches, preaching the same message in two languages, and working with two different leadership boards. The pastor also needs to be accessible to many people from both congregations. The inevitability of burnout is very high in this model. If the pastor ever becomes ill or is away for any period of time, both congregations will be pastor-less. Another important consideration is that this kind of model is not easily transferable or reproducible at the leadership level for the future. The model makes it difficult to prepare leaders because few leaders have the ability to preach in two languages or the energy to oversee two congregations. The better model for leadership may be the biblical prescription of a plurality of leaders as seen with elders and deacons (Phil 1:1; 1 Tim 3:1–13). The plurality model will solve many of the concerns outlined above by empowering different leaders with different gifts to reach and shepherd all the people in the two congregations. At best, the 2-in-1 model is a short-term model that does not look promising for the future.

Conclusion

While this chapter has given a quick overview of the nine different church models that Asian Americans attend, I need to make a few general and crucial observations for a better understanding of the Asian American church movement.

The Need for the Asian American Church

A recent study showed that Orange County, California, has the third largest Asian American population in the United States,[10] with over 600,000 Asians and Asian Americans living in that area. This is astounding! But one only needs to go into a city such as Irvine, California, for example, to see the many restaurants, businesses, markets, and churches that have Asian writing somewhere on the signage. Whether the population is religious or not is yet to be seen. But given the often strong cultural trait of religion within these cultures, it is not surprising that more and more Asian American churches are being formed and planted within this area.

The Cyclical Nature of the Church Models

It is important to note that there is no one best church model. In other words, one model is not necessarily better than the other. They are just different. What this means is that one model may be a better fit than another depending on the needs of the members of the congregation. Now having

10. http://www.latimes.com/local/orangecounty/la-me-asian-oc-20140714-story.html.

said this, I also need to note that there is a cyclical nature or progression of the models based on the age and growth of the church. When a church begins in its early stage, it may be a Room-for-Let model. When the English members get older and more financially stable, they may be able to sustain a Duplex model. This in turn can lead to a Townhouse or Independent Church model years later as the English congregation is older and mature enough to lead a church. All of this is natural and to be expected as the members mature and get older.

The Most Important Point about Church Models!

Finally, it must be said that the models, in and of themselves, do not make the church. They are just one part of the success of a church. What is also necessary for the success of the church is not the models themselves but the people who lead and make up the church. This means that men and women of godly character and virtue are necessary for any church to work regardless of the church model, the ethnicity of the membership, or the denominational affiliation. In terms of character, especially for leaders, the qualifications listed in 1 Tim 3:1–13 and Titus 1:4–9 are essentials for godly and biblical leadership. In terms of virtues, love, patience, humility, and grace are also essential in regards to relating well to one another. But again, both the model and the quality of the people are a must for the church to flourish and succeed. For it is possible to have a good church model but not-so-good people leading it. This will lead to ruin. On the flip side, a church could have wonderful people, and no clue on how to structure a model of church. That scenario will also prove to be a disaster. A good blend of godly leadership and an appropriate church model, however, is an example of the both/and or yin/yang balance of harmony that will be a good recipe for success for the Asian American church of the future.

In the next chapter we will explore the concept of shame as it influences Asian Americans, noting similarities with the first-century Christians, and discuss how God has covered and removed our shame.

Reflection Questions

1. Which model of church did you grow up in as a child? What are some of your memories (both good and bad) of this type of church?

2. Which model of church seems most appealing to you long-term and why?

3. Which model of church seems to be the most "biblical"? Briefly explain.

4. Spend twenty minutes reflecting on Acts 6:1–7, 10:34–35, and 11:19–26 and write down what God is speaking to you about as a result of reflecting on these issues.

2

Ain't That a Shame

Introduction

ONE OF THE ESSENTIAL concepts within the Asian American culture of today is the idea of shame. Shame, along with its positive counterpart honor, is found throughout Asian and Asian American culture. It is closely related to the individual, the family, and the church. The Asian concept of shame has many similarities with Greco-Roman first-century practices seen in the New Testament. We can draw many parallels between the two cultures and learn many lessons by simply comparing the two cultures. As we study the cultural patterns and historical lessons from the first-century Greco-Roman culture, we can, with God's help, correct practices in twenty-first-century Asian American society. This chapter will demonstrate the correlation of the biblical lessons related to shame in light of the framework of Roman cultural practices as they relate to modern twenty-first-century Asian American spiritual tendencies. It will also show how Jesus became the ultimate Shame-Bearer by taking away all of our sin and shame through his death on the cross.

Disobedience Brings Shame into the World

Shame can be traced back to the Fall. Genesis 2–3 gives us a basis for understanding the effects of sin and shame on all mankind as it was originally shown through Adam and Eve. We see that Adam and Eve were placed within the perfect state of the Garden of Eden. No sin, no hardship, no shame anywhere in this perfect paradise. Relationally, there was no strife, nor any problems between Adam and Eve or even between humans and God. We are also told in Gen 2:25 that "the man and his wife were both naked and were not ashamed." This is an indication of the positive state of a world that had yet to be affected by sin and its consequences.

Yet Adam and Eve's disposition changed quickly as they both succumbed to temptation and ate of the fruit of the tree of the knowledge of good and evil (Gen 2:6). Their disobedience, in turn, led them to hide themselves due to shame. For the first time, Adam and Eve both realized evil. We see then in Gen 3:7 that "the eyes of both were opened, and they knew that they were naked. And they sewed fig leaves together and made themselves loincloths." Sin had entered into the world, and one of the first effects of sin was manifested. This experience introduced shame and its negative consequences.

We clearly see how sin and shame affected both Adam and Eve by looking at their responses. There are typically two responses or results that come from shame: 1) hiding/fear and 2) blaming / blame shifting. The first example of hiding is seen in Gen 3:8–10, when God is walking in the garden calling out to Adam. This was a normal, daily practice of fellowship and relationship building between God and his creation. But at the end of verse 8, we see that "the man and his wife hid themselves from the presence of the LORD God among the trees of the garden." Further, we see that God calls out to Adam in verse 9 asking, "Where are you?" This is not a question indicating that God didn't know where Adam was but rather an invitation to meet with Adam because he was hiding from God. We see Adam's response to God's call in Gen 3:10 where he says, "I heard the sound of you in the garden, and I was *afraid*, because I was *naked*, and I *hid* myself." All of these dynamics were indicative of shame and were clear manifestations of hiding and fear. God responds to Adam in verse 11 asking him, "Who told you that you were naked? Have you eaten of the tree of which I commanded you not to eat?" God asks Adam directly about his realization of his nakedness. There is a stark contrast between the pre-Fall situation when Adam and Eve were not ashamed of their nakedness (Gen 2:25) and their post-Fall attempts to cover themselves due to their shame (Gen 3:7).

The second blatant result of shame comes in the form of blaming or blame shifting (Gen 3:11–13). After Adam is confronted by God in Gen 3:11, he gives the classic response in Gen 3:12. When Adam was asked if he had disobeyed God, Adam responds by blaming Eve saying, "The *woman* whom *you* gave to be with me, *she* gave me the fruit of the tree, and I ate." Rather than taking full ownership of his sin, Adam blames God and the woman for his situation. Adam finally takes partial responsibility with his final admission: ". . . and I ate." But this was only after he had blamed both the woman and God as the main reasons for his sin. Similarly, Eve followed suit in verse 13. When the woman was confronted by God for her sin, her response is "The serpent deceived me, and I ate." Notice that in each case, the blame was put on someone else first and later followed by a soft admission of ". . . and I ate." Adam and Eve eventually made a personal admission, but only after they shifted blame away from their own behavior.

These two responses, hiding and blaming, are endemic to all people and cultures but are found more prominently within Asian American contexts due to the strong level of shame in the culture. Due to the other dynamic of honor, there typically are many family secrets that are hidden from the public eye in order to avoid the possibility of shaming the family name. Issues such as financial troubles have left families embarrassed to ask for help and often end tragically in entire family suicides. Such suicides are an extreme example of shame felt by the family. Another frequent problem seen especially in the Asian American church is when married couples face struggles and hardships. Rather than asking for help and counsel, couples often hide the problem and it doesn't surface until divorce papers are served. In marital difficulties hiding and blaming are both prevalent.

One such marital situation happened to me years ago when I pastored married couples in my ministry. Our couples group met every other Sunday for nearly a year to do Bible study, to have fellowship, and to give accountability to one another. After the ministry ended, a number of couples suddenly left the church. A fellow pastor friend at another church asked me why these folks had suddenly showed up at his church. At the time, I suggested that they were possibly only visiting. Then he alerted me that the couple had actually applied for membership within his church. When I heard this, I called each husband and asked if everything was all right, and if they were still at church. In each and every case, they responded "yes" and said that everything was great. They all lied to me about the situation because they had actually left the church secretly and told only a few close friends in the congregation. I was shocked.

When the news spread about their departure, it caused a big stir in the church because a number of the people who had left were related to elders and prominent members of the congregation. The elders were alarmed by their children's departure and asked them why they had left. Each couple responded by saying that they had left due to the pastor—me! This was initially shocking because I thought that I was close to each couple, especially since we had been meeting together for a year in our married group Bible study. Soon thereafter a motion was made at the Elder session for me to be fired due to this exodus of the elders' children. The situation looked grim. Suddenly and unexpectedly, another church member called me informing me that a number of these married couples who had left were filing for divorce. Everything made sense. Since these people were long-time members of the church, some even leaders, and were related to elders, prominent leaders in the church, to be divorced would bring much shame to them and to their families. As a result, they hid by leaving the church and they blamed me, the pastor, rather than owning up to their own situation.

Circumstances like these are certainly unfortunate, but they can also be good opportunities for the body of Christ to step in and give accountability and aid for the people involved. Galatians 6:2 calls believers to "bear one another's burdens" as a direct instruction to help out in times of need. Hebrews 3:12 exhorts: "take care, brethren, lest there be in any of you an evil, unbelieving heart, leading you to fall away from the living God." Openness and accountability are essential for all people, of all generations, of all genders, of all ethnicities. This is mandated all throughout the Scriptures. Yet, due to a combination of shame and pride, struggles often go unnoticed.

Shame and Honor

David deSilva, in his book *Honor, Patronage, Kinship, and Purity* explains honor as "his or her conviction that he or she has embodied those actions and qualities that the group values as 'honorable,' as the marks of a valuable person."[1] He continues to explain that "honor is a dynamic and relational concept."[2] It is definitely relational in the sense that the honor comes from the group or community. He writes, "Honor is also the esteem in which a person is held by the group he or she regards as significant others—it is the recognition by the person's group that he or she is a valuable member of that group. In this regard, it is having the respect of others."[3]

In relation to the collectivist-group orientation of shame, deSilva explains that there are two ways that people received honor in the first century: honor was either ascribed by a group or achieved by the individual. A person could receive ascribed honor by birthright, parentage or lineage, or

1. DeSilva, *Honor*, 25.
2. Ibid., 25.
3. Ibid., 25.

34

by grants bestowed by people of higher status or power.[4] Achieved honor could be won or lost through the challenge and riposte social game that resembled a debate. Jesus often engaged in this type of social interaction with the Pharisees and other Jewish groups.

The main focus of this chapter will be on shame. Shame is the dynamic that works counter to honor. When a person is not honored, they will feel shame. David deSilva writes, "shame signifies, in the first instance, being seen as less than valuable because one has behaved in ways that run contrary to the values of the group."[5]

Kaufman writes, "to feel shame is to feel seen in a painfully diminished sense."[6] Grace Sangalang adds:

> Shame is concerned with both the social aspects of status in our relationship with others, but also, in our relationship with God, and our own view of ourselves as having an intrinsic "badness." This sense results in our tendency to hide and cover the negative parts of ourselves which keeps us from authenticity with God and others.[7]

Shame is complex and includes multiple aspects. Unlike guilt, shame appears as a predominant dynamic within the culture of the first century as well as in global perspective today. Joe Hellerman notes that "ideas about honor and shame can be found in virtually all societies."[8] DeSilva further notes:

> Honor and dishonor, then, are not only about the individual's sense of worth but also about the coordination and promotion of a group's defining and central values, about the strategies for the preservation of a group's culture in the midst of a complex web of competing cultures, and about the ways in which honor or dishonor are attained, displayed and enacted.[9]

It can also be asserted that shame is one of the main cultural dynamics of both the Old and New Testament among the respective people groups

4. Ibid., 28.
5. Ibid., 25.
6. Kaufman, *Shame,* 8.
7. Sangalang, *Wall of Shame,* 8.
8. Hellerman, *Reconstructing Honor,* 35.
9. DeSilva, *Despising Shame,* 42.

of the Bible.[10] While Western cultures focus on guilt, the majority of the world today functions under the shame dynamic. This can be attributed to the other cultural dynamics that work in tandem with shame, i.e., the hierarchical nature of people groups along with the collectivist mentality of different ethnic groups around the world.[11] The prevalence of shame is certainly true for most Asian cultures.

For example, Jackson Wu, in his book *Saving God's Face: A Chinese Contextualization of Salvation through Honor and Shame,* discusses the concept of "losing face." Wu writes, "face is a Chinese way of talking about honor and shame."[12] Wu gives many different terms and definitions for face including claim, identity, social standing, status, one's situated identity, and other-directed self-esteem. He further explains, "face must be protected and given in order to maintain harmony in a group."[13] Also that "one's face is contingent on one's role within a group and the expectations of the community."[14] He concludes that "the concept of shame permeates every aspect of Chinese life."[15] This description sounds very much like the Greco-Roman culture of the first century.

Shame and Guilt

The concept of guilt is found in the New Testament, but not to the degree of the dynamic of shame. Guilt is mentioned through two main Greek words: *enochos* "guilty," found ten times in seven passages (Matt 5:21; 26:26; Mark 3:29; 14:14; 1 Cor 11:27; Heb 2:15; Jas 2:10) and *aitia* "guilt/charge/reason," which is found in twenty passages (Matt 19:3; 19:10; 27:37; Mark 15:26; Luke 8:47; John 18:38; 19:4, 6; Acts 10:21; 13:28; 22:24; 23:28; 25:18; 25:27; 28:18, 20; 2 Tim 1:6, 12; Titus 1:13; Heb 2:11). The number of references to guilt is relatively small compared to the 148 times that shame is mentioned in the Old and New Testaments.

10. Ibid., 24.

11. For an excellent overview of the different cultures of the world, see Sheryl Takagi Silzer's book *Biblical Multicultural Teams* (Pasadena, CA: William Carey International University Press, 2011).

12. Wu, *Saving God's Face,* 151.

13. Ibid., 152.

14. Ibid., 152.

15. Ibid., 153.

So how are guilt and shame different from one another? It is important to realize that there is a significant and qualitative difference between the two. Guilt is pictured through a Western perspective as a court transaction which is addressed in a linear manner. Stockitt writes about how the predominant term for guilt "has consumed the energies of theologians—at least in the Western theological tradition—has been 'guilt,' and this metaphor has defined, shaped, and molded subsequent theological reflection as a result."[16] He further defines guilt by saying, "When sin is defined principally as a transgression against an abstract law then the resultant legal status of the one who has committed the transgression is one of guilt."[17] Stockitt contrasts shame with guilt by suggesting that the nature of shame is inherently relational. He adds, "Shame does not carry a legal meaning in the way guilt appears to. It sounds far more personal, more existential, more corporate."[18] This would be consistent with how shame is typically understood and defined by most scholars of other disciplines.

So how should shame be defined? There are multiple definitions for shame. The definition depends on the discipline and the perspective. A popular vulnerability counselor, Dr. Brene Brown, in her book *Daring Greatly,* defines shame as "the intensely painful feeling or experience of believing that we are flawed and therefore unworthy of love and belonging."[19] Christian author and ethicist Lewis Smedes, in his book *Shame and Grace: Healing the Shame We Don't Deserve,* writes, "Shame is a very heavy feeling. It is a feeling that we do not measure up and maybe never will measure up to the sorts of persons we are meant to be."[20] Robin Stockitt, a minister in the Anglican church, writes:

> Shame can be understood, therefore, as arising from the external pressure of a group, where the use of shame as a social sanction is particularly effective. Shame is closely related to the reception of approval, strikes at the core of who a person is. Shame and anxiety thus become inseparable companions. The fear of being shamed leads to a state of anxious anticipation, which in turn leads to a whole range of coping mechanisms being established.[21]

16. Stockitt, *Restoring the Shamed*, 43.
17. Ibid., 43.
18. Ibid., 44.
19. Brene Brown, *Daring Greatly*, 69.
20. Smedes, *Shame and Grace*, 5.
21. Stockitt, *Restoring the Shamed*, 41.

Social scientist Halvor Moxnes elaborates that one of the main character-istics of an honor-and-shame society is that the group is more important than the individual. He states:

> The individual received status from the group. Therefore, rec-ognition and approval from others were important. Interaction between people was characterized by the competition for recogni-tion and the defense of one's own status and honor. To refuse a person's claim for honor was to put the person to shame. The basic notion in all studies of honor and shame is that they represent the value of a person in her or his own eyes but also in the eyes of his or her society.[22]

Finally, Joe Hellerman accounts how honor was preeminently a public com-modity. He states: "In the collectivist culture of antiquity, one's honor was almost exclusively dependent upon the affirmation of the claim to honor by the larger social group to which the individual belonged."[23] For many in the first century, the *cursus honorum* ("court of honors") was a preoccupation of a person's life. This listing gave justification for a person to have honor or not as they were recognized by others in the society.

Paul's Perspectives of Shame and Approval

Throughout the Apostle Paul's letters, he gives many examples of honor and shame. Paul uses either the term "shame" or "ashamed" a total of twenty times in his letters. The Greek words are either *kataischune* or *entropen*, used interchangeably for "shame" (1 Cor 1:27; 4:14; 6:5; 11:22; 15:34; 2 Cor 4:2; 7:14; 9:4; 10:8; 11:21; Phil 1:20; 3:19; 2 Thess 3:14; Titus 2:8) and *epaisc-hunomai* for "ashamed" (Rom 1:16; 6:21; 2 Tim 1:8, 12, 16; 2:15).

This concept of shame is often accompanied by the term for "approv-al" or "approved." The Greek word *dokimos* "approved" is used throughout Paul's writing (Rom 14:18; 16:10; 1 Cor 10:18; 11:19; 13:7; 2 Cor 10:18; 2 Tim 2:15). Paul clearly identifies the source of his higher approval in 1 Thess 2:4 when he writes, ". . . but just as we have been approved by God to be entrusted with the gospel, so we speak, not as pleasing men, but God who examines our hearts." This concept of approval relates to shame in two Roman practices that will be mentioned in the next section.

22. Moxnes, "Honor," 208.

23. Hellerman, *Reconstructing Honor*, 35.

First-Century Roman Culture and
Twenty-first-Century Asian Culture

There are uncanny similarities between first-century Roman culture and twenty-first-century Asian American culture. The similarities manifest through specific practices that relate to honor and shame. Many of the similarities can be attributed to the fact that both cultures are hierarchical in nature and demonstrate collectivism to differing degrees. We will examine two specific practices in the two cultures that parallel each other closely: the court of reputation and the *cursus honorum*. These practices, although ancient in nature, seem to have parallels in the twenty-first-century practices within Asian American religious and spiritual experiences. When upheld, these practices would bring great honor. When these practices failed, they would be cause for shame.

One of the common first-century Roman practices was something called the court of reputation. David deSilva defines this group as "that body of significant others whose 'opinion' about what is honorable and shameful, and whose evaluation of the individual, really matters."[24] This group functioned in a way that is described as the "eyes" that needed to "be directed toward one another, toward their leaders, and, frequently, toward beings beyond the visible sphere (for example, God or the honored members of the group who have moved to another realm after death) as they look for approval."[25] The opinion of this court of reputation factored heavily into the individual's decision-making, for either approval or disapproval for different issues. This facet of the collectivist mindset of Asian Americans, for example, can provide a cultural pressure to do what is "right" in the eyes of the group for purposes of conformity or harmony.

Within this cultural framework, the individual is highly dependent on the group's collective approval. But as this concept extends into the Christian's life, there is someone who is greater than the group who needs to give approval. That person is God. This issue is discussed by deSilva as he writes, "Most prominent within this court of reputation is God, whose central place is assured because of God's power to enforce his estimation of who deserves honor and who merits censure."[26] This value is affirmed by the Apostle Paul throughout his ministry and his writings when he notes that

24. DeSilva, *Despising Shame,* 40.
25. Ibid., 40.
26. Ibid., 55.

the approval of God is more important than that of any person or people group. Again, Paul makes this clear when he states, ". . . but just as we have been approved by God to be entrusted with the gospel, so we speak, not as pleasing men, but God who examines our hearts" (1 Thess 2:4).

In the Asian American culture and community, a strong parallel "court of reputation" includes parents, elders in a church, the pastor, peers, and anyone else who is watching the believer, especially the person giving approval (or disapproval) and has a title. This takes many shapes in terms of decisions and final outcomes. For example, when a young man commits himself to the Lord in a serious manner, he is often encouraged to go to seminary for further training. The decision is often made by a pastor, parents, older authorities, and sometimes even by peers. While this practice may prove to be a positive experience, sometimes it becomes detrimental to the young man if he does not have a "calling" or desire for full-time ministry from the Lord. A biblical example of a personal calling may be seen in 1 Tim 3:1 which states, "If any man aspires to the office of overseer, it is a fine work *he* desires to do." The point is that sometimes the "court of reputation" gives a person an obligation instead of a clear calling that comes directly from the Lord.

The "court of reputation" can also function as a positive influence and peer pressure to help maintain high levels of piety, holiness, and spiritual discipline. This is done when the group engages all together in activities such as morning prayer, Bible study, a retreat, or a service event. For many Asian American churches, the actual structure of the church may include an older congregation of people who speak the native language. In Chinese churches, the generations are termed Overseas-Born Chinese (OBC) and American-Born Chinese (ABC). For Korean churches, the designations are expressed with numbers. The older first-generation of Korean-speaking people are known as 1.0 generation churches or Korean Ministries (KM), while the younger generation are the 2.0 generation, also called the English Ministries (EM). The "court of reputation" dynamic works well when both generations of the church recognize and acknowledge the work or well-being of a congregation member for either their service or for their contribution to the church. In many ways, this paradigm is established as a means to achieve honor, but more so in order to avoid shame, a matter of great importance in the Asian American culture.

Another Roman practice of the first century was the idea of *cursus honorum*. This term was yet another means for honor to be upheld centered around the honorific offices of the political arena. These "races for honors" showed up in many places including gravestones that would basically list all of the accomplishments of the deceased person. This was the way that a person received honor. This practice can often be seen in a Korean funeral program as well. Hellerman defines the *cursus honorum* as "a sequence of offices that marked the standard career for the Roman senatorial class, and which had been in place since the middle of the fourth century BCE."[27]

Again, the Apostle Paul reflects the first-century Roman culture in his writing in Phil 3:5–6. He follows the typical model of listing his honorable accomplishments, both ascribed and acquired: ". . . circumcised the eighth day; of the nation of Israel, of the tribe of Benjamin, a Hebrew born of Hebrews; regarding the law, a Pharisee; regarding zeal, persecuting the church; regarding righteousness that is in the law, blameless." This would fit perfectly with the *cursus honorum* of the day, especially since Philippi was a colony that was under the rule of the Roman government. But the Apostle Paul doesn't stop with listing his accomplishments. He proceeds in an unexpected direction. After he lists his achievements he states, ". . . more than that, I also consider everything to be a loss in view of the surpassing value of knowing Christ Jesus my Lord." Paul travels the route of humility just like his Lord Jesus Christ. This is quite an unexpected turn culturally speaking because it is very counter-cultural to go in this direction. Again Paul shifts the direction of approval to a higher source and, in this case, it was that of knowing the Lord Jesus Christ.

Years ago, at a large conference for Asian American college students, a speaker who was invited by the organizing group gave a sermon that was very much like a *cursus honorum*. He cited his many accomplishments academically as well as all the high-ranking positions that he had held during his lifetime. It was quite interesting to see the different generational responses to the speaker's message. Some of the older Asian Americans were awed by how accomplished and prominent the speaker was based on his many years of ministry. The younger Asian Americans, however, were totally disgusted with his talk because they perceived it to be a shallow boasting of personal accomplishments that seemed both inappropriate and unnecessary as it was simply seen as arrogant boasting. This reaction from the younger generation led to an emergency meeting of the organizers, who voted to have the oldest member of the group confront the speaker about his inappropriate boasting. I was the chosen spokesperson. As the

27. Hellerman, *Reconstructing Honor*, 51.

"rebuke" was occurring, the speaker received everything very graciously and changed his approach. I now realize that it may have been too premature and even incorrect to judge his motives as negative. He was just establishing his credibility through his modern day *cursus honorum*.

Another example of the practice of *cursus honorum* within Asian American religious and spiritual experiences is the practice of acquiring academic degrees to bolster one's standing or credibility. At a seminary, this is minimally done through working towards a Masters of Divinity degree. A generation ago, the MDiv was the most popular degree that was needed to become a pastor, a position of status and honor. While this has changed in the larger Western culture in America, it still remains true among Asian American students and workers. For many American churches, a Master's degree in New Testament, which is significantly shorter in terms of academic units, is often sufficient for a person to become a pastor. In some cases, a degree may not even be required for some denominations and churches. This is not the case for Asian Americans. Part of the desire for the MDiv degree can be attributed to the "court of reputation," which encourages students to achieve more learning and some of it can be attributed to the student, who is building his *cursus honorum*. Some of these same students go on to work towards additional degrees such as a Masters of Theology (ThM), Doctor of Ministry (DMin), and even Doctor of Philosophy (PhD). The academic degrees certainly exceed the job requirements but they do strengthen the honor status for the pastor or leader. Social historian Joe Hellerman notes:

> Traditional Asian culture is wedded to honor and shame in much the same way as the ancient Roman culture was. Instead of public offices in a *cursus honorum*, however, today's Koreans regard educational achievements and vocational status as the key criteria for honor in the public sphere.[28]

The effect of shame typically leads to withdrawal and hiding oneself, but withdrawal/hiding can be accomplished in more than one way. For example, Stockitt notes:

> . . . for some it is camouflaged by an excess of pious spirituality; for others by resignation. We go to extraordinary lengths to run away from this disease of the soul, by denying it is there, by refusing to stop, by filling every corner of our lives with busyness, hoping that the dread feeling will simply drift away and disappear.[29]

28. Hellerman, *Embracing Shared Ministry*, 138.
29. Stockitt, *Restoring the Shamed*, 6.

The tendency for Asian American Christians would then be to engross themselves in religious piety, service, or activity to gain approval (from human authority or from God himself), through good works which are actually motivated by shame. For example, the *cursus honorum* can be viewed as a list of accomplishments that may be interpreted as a means to give back to God through service or various positions that are held in the church. This "more is better" worldview is prevalent among Asian Americans as they sometimes tend to quantify their spirituality. For Korean Americans, this may be seen through early morning prayer, longer prayers, louder prayers, bigger church buildings, and greater fervor in one's spirituality.

The combination of the modern day "court of reputation" with the *cursus honorum* pressure can drive a person in an Asian culture to feel great shame, especially if he feels that he is not doing an adequate job in performing the tasks and duties which would be considered excellent. This kind of drive can lead to other potentially unhealthy attitudes and conditions, including obsessive-compulsive behavior and detached emotions, which can culminate in burnout and fatigue. Burnout can affect a person's spiritual condition significantly, even to the point of abandoning one's faith. That is why there needs to be good accountability and monitoring of our spiritual and emotional health.

In light of these parallels between first-century Roman culture and twenty-first-century Asian American culture, we need to remember that we should seek approval from God rather than from people. This was the Apostle Paul's point and what the Scripture as a whole would emphasize for believers today. Even though some of the practices of the court of reputation and the *cursus honorum* may prove beneficial, a person still needs to check his own motives and heart before the Lord so that he can wholeheartedly make the choices that would be honorable to God.

Other Struggles and Hardships that Asian Americans Face

Shame definitely has a strong residual effect on Asian Americans. Shame can impact the quality of ministries such as small groups, significantly restricting the openness and sharing of the group. Thus, many small groups struggle with going deeper and connecting with each other. This kind of shame carries into other areas as well. Many times, leaders, due to shame, are isolated from others and thus lack accountability. Adding to this dynamic is the whole hierarchical nature of the Asian culture that prevents younger people from even questioning leaders. This shame-based practice is contrary to passages such as 1 Tim 5:1, where Paul encourages young Timothy to "not sharply rebuke an older man but appeal to him as a father."[30] This means that respect and honor must accompany the accountability. The "how" here is just as important as the "what."

Failure is yet another area in which many Asian Americans feel shame. So much can be learned by openly sharing failure, because it can serve as a "back door to success." Years ago, as I was studying for my comprehensive exam for my Masters in Theology, I ended up failing two of the five sections. I had become too busy with too many tasks and I didn't study well for the exam. I thought that both my graduation and my future job as a professor would be jeopardized. Fortunately, the dean of the seminary at the time was gracious to give me another opportunity. I was able to retake the exam, pass with flying colors, graduate, and begin teaching at the seminary shortly after. Now, I often share this story in class because it gives the students a glimpse of how to respond to and recover from failure. I saw the failure as just an isolated event and not as a part of my identity.

Jesus, Our Ultimate Shame Bearer

For followers of Christ, the solution to our shame and the restoration of our honor is found at the cross. Hebrews 12:2–3 tells us:

> . . . looking to Jesus, the founder and perfecter of our faith, who for the joy that was set before him endured the cross, despising the shame, and is seated at the right hand of the throne of God. Consider him who endured from sinners such hostility against himself, so that you may not grow weary or faint-hearted.

Jesus took all of mankind's sin and shame upon himself and took them away. He exchanged the sin with grace and the shame with honor. Sangalang writes, "Because Christ took the ultimate shame upon himself on the cross, he inverted the notion of shame as the cross, which was supposed to be a place of great shame, became a place of honor."[31]

So what exactly does it mean that Christ took our shame and gave us honor instead? The event that demonstrates this transaction is the

30. *NASB*, 1995.
31. Sangalang, *Wall of Shame*, 7.

crucifixion of Christ on the cross. There are at least four transactions involved in this important act. Jesus did the following for us: 1) he carried the cross publicly, allowing for openness amidst injustice; 2) he was mocked and beaten, taking our pain; 3) he was given the crown of thorns, absorbing our disgrace; and 4) finally, he was crucified, laying to rest all the shame.

In first-century Roman times, to carry one's cross was an excruciating process. It involved physical, emotional, and psychological pain. The cross was carried in public through the streets as a means of showing admission of a crime (Luke 23:26). In an honor and shame culture, this act by itself would bring incredible shame to the person carrying the cross. Amazingly, Jesus, who was innocent on all counts, did this shameful act on behalf of all sinners. Publically carrying the cross was the beginning of the exchange in which he took our shame and replaced it with his honor. Jesus publicly bore the shame of the cross, openly showing the injustice of the situation. The example of Jesus allows us to be open with our shame as well, especially if we have been victims of something unjust. It gives us permission and empowerment to face our shame. As Jesus was then placed on the cross, he continued to take all of the shame of mankind upon himself by receiving all the abuse that people gave him. We read that he was mocked (Luke 23:38) and beaten (John 19:32) by the soldiers. A sarcastic inscription "This is the King of the Jews" (Luke 23:38) was placed over him on the cross. This all must have been very painful to bear, yet Jesus took all of this on our behalf. He took all of our pain and abuse. Abuse included the crown of thorns placed on Jesus' head (Matt 27:29). Not only was this the ultimate mockery of the kingship of Jesus, it was also an agonizing reminder that Jesus absorbed all the shame and disgrace on our behalf. Finally, right before Jesus gave up his last breath, he cried out with the loud words, "It is finished" (John 19:30). The exchange from shame to honor was completely restored through the crucifixion on the cross.

Conclusion

This last emphasis on Christ's death and his crucifixion is essential in knowing that shame was crucified on the cross. Theologically, we see that a number of passages infer this from different angles. Jesus stated, "It is finished" in John 19:30, bringing closure to his atoning work. The writer of Hebrews writes, "And by that will we have been sanctified through the offering of the body of Jesus Christ once for all" (Heb 10:10). Peter tells us, "He himself bore our sins in his body on the tree, that we might die to sin and live to righteousness. By his wounds you have been healed" (1 Pet 2:24). John assures us, "If we confess our sins, he is faithful and just to forgive us our sins and to cleanse us from all unrighteousness" (1 John 1:9). We need to believe these truths because they all claim the effects of the finished work of Christ on the cross. Our shame has been taken away and has been crucified.

As a result, because of Christ's work on the cross, the exchange moves from shame to honor due to Christ. We share honor with Christ as co-heirs with him. Romans 8:17 states, ". . . and if children, then heirs—heirs of God and fellow heirs with Christ, provided we suffer with him in order that we may also be glorified with him." We will also receive glory in the form of a crown. First Peter 5:4 declares, "And when the chief Shepherd appears, you will receive the unfading crown of glory." Paul affirms these honors again in Eph 2:6 as we are "raised up with him and seated us with him in the heavenly places in Christ Jesus." Finally, in 1 Cor 15:54, we see that "death is swallowed up in victory." As children of God, we are thankful that the shame was taken away by Christ and we look forward in eager anticipation to the honor and glory of our Lord Jesus Christ!

Our shame often prevents us from being able to accept God's grace. In the next chapter we discuss differences between what I call "Western Grace" and "Global Grace" and show how both kinds of grace can give us a more complete picture of God's grace.

Reflection Questions

1. Why might knowing the difference between shame and guilt be helpful? Explain.

2. What aspects of shame affect you the most in your Christian life?

3. As you reflect on Jesus, our Ultimate Shame-Bearer, how does this dimension of his death on the cross give you hope?

4. Read Phil 2:5-11; Rom 8:12–18; and Heb 12:1–3 keeping in your mind the dynamics of honor and shame. Write down some thoughts about what God is showing you about your relationship with him.

3

Grace Is More Than a Korean Girl's Name

Introduction

TRADITIONALLY, THE NAME "GRACE" is a very common name given to Korean girls. The popularity of the name may be due a family's Christian values, history, and possible church connections. Grace is a central doctrine of the Christian faith (Eph 2:8–10). This term has commonly been defined in Christian circles as "an unmerited favor." While this statement is not false, it does not explain the full extent of the depth and breadth of the concept of grace. This chapter will demonstrate different cultural and historical meanings of grace and will also show the overlap between the first-century idea of patronage and the twenty-first-century practice of grace in Asian American circles today. In addition, I will also introduce and differentiate two new terms: Western Grace (WG) and Global Grace (GG) and show how they are different in concept and in practice.

Some Misunderstandings about Grace

Many twentieth-century Bible scholars have suggested that the concept of grace was a limited one that could only be found in the New Testament. They base their suggestion on a separation between Law for the Old Testament and grace for the New Testament. One well-known proponent of this view is C.I. Scofield, a traditional dispensational theologian. He made this dichotomy in the notes of his Scofield Reference Bible (1917) by suggesting that Old Testament saints were saved by the Law and New Testament saints by grace. Scofield writes, "As a dispensation, grace begins with the death and resurrection of Christ . . . The point of testing is no longer legal obedience as the condition of salvation, but acceptance or rejection of Christ, with good works as the fruit of salvation."[1]

Scofield's separation of law and grace has been both the depiction and the critique of the traditional dispensational framework of theology. In this system, there was a clear separation between the dispensation of *Law* in the Old Testament and the dispensation of *Grace* in the New Testament. Within this separation, the assumption was that grace was absent from the Old Testament and was only a New Testament practice. This division has been shown to be false and has even been clarified with the updated version of progressive dispensationalism.

Traditional Reformed theologians, who hold to the Lutheran perspective of Paul, have also viewed the Old Covenant as devoid of grace and the New Covenant as full of grace. This distinction was a key component within this system of theology that distinguished between the "works of the law" of the Old Covenant and the "gospel of grace" within the New Covenant. Foundational books such as Romans and Galatians were used as biblical support for this theological distinction. This view has been the traditional, evangelical understanding of grace.

Many of these previous views have been challenged by more recent studies and scholarship on this subject. For example, the New Perspective of Paul, made famous by scholars such as E.P. Sanders, James Dunn, and N.T. Wright, have correctly identified that "grace" can be found all throughout Judaism and the Old Testament. An example of this type of grace can be found in the Hebrew word *hesed,* which is translated "lovingkindness" in passages such as Lam 3:22. Other terms, such as "favor" or *chen,* are also used throughout the Old Testament in passages such as Ezra 9:8, Ps 45:2, and Ps 84:11. Ronald M. Hals, in his book *Grace and Faith in the Old Testament,* writes, "The confession and celebration of God's gracious acts is a major emphasis in the Old Testament."[2]

First-Century Roman Understanding of Grace

Historically, as well as culturally, grace, has also been known by the term patronage, which was a prevalent dynamic within the first-century Roman society. While the modern understanding of the word patronage has some negative connotations, the ancient world viewed patronage as a positive

---

1. Scofield Reference Bible, 1115.
2. Hals, *Grace and Faith,* 21.

and necessary requirement for survival. David deSilva notes that within the Roman world, patronage was a means "to access goods, protection, or opportunities for employment and advancement."[3] A patron-client relationship was essential to Roman society, because of the limited access to goods, advancement, and even survival.

Under this construct, the patron or benefactor would typically be an individual with substantial wealth and resources. The client would be someone who needed safety, protection, goods, or food. One of the most common examples of this exchange would be between a wealthy king or ruler who would provide for an entire city or province. The patronage relationship would result in a number of advantages for the patron as well as for the client. The patron would be honored for having a good name and reputation for being generous and kind. The client would receive resources and, in turn. would respond by giving public recognition to the patron by publicly honoring and supporting him. As a result, the client was to respond by being loyal and by being willing to provide any and all services to help the patron. This practice exemplifies the reciprocity that was common in the culture of patronage. Just as the patron was a graceful giver, so should the client be a graceful responder. This concept carries over into the New Testament with Jesus as the patron and the followers of Christ as the clients. The practice of patronage can also be seen all throughout Asian culture, as will be explored shortly.

Jesus Christ was the ultimate patron in history who superseded the cultural norm of the first century. David deSilva explains that in the New Testament "they would have understood that Christ was the broker, or mediator, which connected clients to access God's favor in dying for them (Rom 5:8)."[4] This act of Christ, dying on the cross, is the ultimate act of patronage. God, being the greatest benefactor of grace, supplies mankind, the clients, with salvation, through the person of Christ. This in turn sets up all believers (clients) to give back to God as gracious responders to God who is the gracious giver to all who believe. Part of the reciprocation would be obedience, loyalty, service, worship, and faithfulness by the followers of Christ.

Once this grace-gift is given to clients, the natural response for them is to give back to both the patron (God) and to others, fellow believers. John 14:15 shows an example of giving back to God when John writes, "If you

3. DeSilva, *Honor,* 19.
4. Ibid., 130.

love me, you will keep my commandments." Giving or charity to others can also be seen in 2 Cor 9:13 where Paul writes, "By their approval of this service, they will glorify God because of your submission that comes from your confession of the gospel of Christ, and the generosity of your contribution for them and for all others." While these examples demonstrate the responsibility of believers to Christ, it should be noted that even in the larger secular society, grace is also shown through acts of kindness given to others by the concept of "paying it forward." Pay it forward is an expression for describing the beneficiary of a good deed repaying it to others instead of to the original benefactor. Theologians refer to this practice as part of pre-venient grace, a much larger movement of God that affects the entire world, both believers and unbelievers, as grace is infused into a general morality throughout humankind. As a result, whether believer or unbeliever, grace was known, seen, and felt by all.

Is Grace Unilateral or Bilateral?

Most Western theologians state that grace is a unilateral experience of God to humankind. In other words, grace is free, with no strings attached. Reformed theologians would strongly contest anything other than this kind of grace. However, unilateral grace does not seem to be the case according to the many examples in antiquity. One of the most recent works that has challenged this traditional understanding of grace is John Barclay's massive work *Paul and the Gift*. In his work, Barclay gives an overview of the concept of grace as a gift viewed from the first century to the twenty-first century. Barclay states, "But even the slightest knowledge of antiquity would inform us that gifts were given with strong expectations of return—indeed, precisely in order to elicit a return and thus to create or enhance social solidarity."[5]

So it seems that not only in antiquity, but also globally, grace has more of a bilateral nature to it. In other words, the necessity of reciprocity is inherent in the idea of grace. In order to better understand and distinguish the differences between these two kinds of graces, I have coined the terms *Global Grace* (GG) and *Western Grace* (WG). Basically, Global Grace is a bilateral reciprocation of a gift from the client back to the patron. This type of reciprocal practice clearly resonates with Asian Americans from the twenty-first century as well as with the first-century practice of patronage.

5. Barclay, *Paul*, 11.

This Global Grace is different from Western Grace, which is only unilateral in nature. Western Grace would be the equivalent to the evangelical Lutheran understanding of grace that has emerged from the Reformation period. Thus, Western Grace can only be traced back to the sixteenth-century Reformation time at the earliest. While this understanding of grace has been widely held by Western Evangelicals, the recent scholarship by John Barclay has challenged this view. His study concludes that the Western Grace understanding may not be a true reflection of the practices of the first century. Rather, Global Grace may be a better portrayal of grace because it is in alignment with the cultural idea of patronage. This new perspective has become a hotly debated issue in theological studies and has the potential to bring a greater understanding of grace to Western Evangelicalism. In order to better understand the differences, this next section will highlight Western Grace (WG) and its unilateral nature.

Unilateral Western Grace (WG)

Much of the discussion related to grace is that it is unmerited, free from debt, and comes "with no strings attached." In other words, is grace only unilateral in nature? Lewis Sperry Chafer, founder of Dallas Theological Seminary, states this view clearly:

> Grace means pure unrecompensed kindness and favor. What is done in grace is done graciously. From this exact meaning there can be no departure; otherwise grace ceases to be grace.[6]

Chafer continues to explain the nature of grace with seven fundamental facts about grace. He further clarifies the unilateral nature of grace under his third point that is entitled "Grace Cannot Incur a Debt." In this section, Chafer emphasizes that grace is purely a gift or a favor that is a pure benefit from God. He then states the following regarding the unilateral nature of grace:

> And, in like manner, no service is to be wrought, and no offering is to be given, with a view to repaying God for his gift. Any attempt to compensate God for his gift is an act so utterly out of harmony with the revealed Truth, and exhibits such a lack of appreciation of his loving bounty, that it cannot be other than distressing to the Giver. All attempts to repay his gift, be they ever so sincere, serve

6. Chafer, *Grace*, 4.

only to frustrate his grace and to lower the marvelous kindness
of God to the sordid level of barter and trade. How faithfully we
should serve Him, but never to repay Him![7]

At many levels, Chafer is correct in his analysis of this doctrine of grace. On
the other hand, much of what he asserts would go against both the culture
of the New Testament as well as some texts within the Scriptures that actually point to the reciprocal and bilateral nature of grace.

Another well-known example of Western Grace (WG) is demonstrated by Dr. John Piper in his book *Future Grace*. In an effort to show how
grace is free, Piper makes the following statement about something he calls
the "Debtor's Ethic." Piper writes:

> The debtor's ethic says, "Because you have done something good
> for me, I feel indebted to do something good for you." This im-
> pulse is not what gratitude was designed to produce. God meant
> gratitude to be a spontaneous expression of pleasure in the gift
> and the good will of another. He did not mean it to be an impulse
> to return favors. If gratitude is twisted into a sense of debt, it gives
> birth to the debtor's ethic—and the effect is to nullify grace.[8]

While it is clear that Piper's intent is to defend the purity of grace and to
give credit to God for his provision, he disregards the cultural and historical evidence of how grace was shown through patronage. Both in antiquity
and globally, bilateral grace has been the norm. Grace has always been reciprocal in nature. To not return grace with grace would be to shame the
person who is giving. This reciprocal nature of grace will be discussed from
a historical and from a scriptural perspective.

Bilateral Global Grace (GG)

The bilateral nature of grace/patronage is evident throughout the Scriptures.
In Heb 12:28, for example, the writer states, "Therefore let us be grateful for
receiving a kingdom that cannot be shaken, and thus let us offer to God
acceptable worship, with reverence and awe." In other words, just as God
has granted his kingdom to believers in Christ, the grateful response to this
gift of grace is worship that is done in reverence and awe. DeSilva clarifies
this by saying, "One of the more important contributions an awareness of

7. Ibid., 7.
8. Piper, *Future Grace*, 32.

the ethos of grace in the first-century world can make is implanting in our minds the necessary connection between giving and responding, between favor and gratitude in the fullest sense."[9]

This cultural backdrop of the New Testament was widely held and understood. This is the context in which the writers of the New Testament wrote. DeSilva continues to explain:

> Because we think about the grace of God through the lens of sixteenth-century Protestant polemics against "earning salvation by means of pious works," we have a difficult time hearing the New Testament's own affirmation of the simple, yet noble and beautiful, circle of grace. God has acted generously, and Jesus has granted great and wonderful gifts. These were not earned, but grace is never earned in the ancient world (this again is not something that sets New Testament grace apart from everyday grace). Once favor has been shown and gifts conferred, however, the result must invariably be that the recipient will show gratitude, will answer grace with grace.[10]

While the Reformed Evangelical concept of grace implies a unilateral without merit type of grace (Western Grace), the biblical text seems to better align with the patronage idea of Global Grace. One of reasons for the fallacious premises of sixteenth-century Reformed theology is that it was a polemic in Europe against Roman Catholicism. Roman Catholicism was seen as a works-based religion by which one could earn salvation through merits and works. As a result, the writings of Luther and Calvin were cast in the light of responding to Roman Catholicism. Thus, the understanding that the works of the Reformation, as valuable as they were, applied mainly to sixteenth-century Europe, not to first-century Asia Minor. The New Perspective, with its cultural emphasis and understanding, lands closer in its depiction of the culture of the first century and of the practice of grace. This next section will highlight some of the important texts about grace using, mainly John's and Paul's writings as examples.

John, in both his Gospel and first epistle, demonstrates examples of the reciprocity of the patron-client type of grace where grace would be understood as something that should be returned. In John 14:15, for example, we see that John states, "If you love Me, you will keep my commandments." The reciprocity here expects that the natural response to loving God will

9. DeSilva, *Honor*, 141.

10. Ibid., 140.

manifest itself in obedience to his commandments. In 1 John 4:19 we read, "We love, because he first loved us." Again, we see that God initiates with his love and that our reciprocal response would be to love him back. Part of our response would be in our worship, in our obedience, and in our relationships with others. To not do so would be unusual, disobedient, and unwarranted. In 1 John 3:16, John extends this love we have for God by giving to others. John writes, "By this we know love, that he laid down his life for us, and we ought to lay down our lives for the brothers." In each and every case, there was some kind of reciprocal response, motivated by grace that is given back to God. There must be a response to God in all of these cases otherwise this would be dishonorable to God, the Giver.

One of the best examples of Global Grace can be seen in the short letter of Philemon. The reciprocity shown here is between Paul and Philemon, who was probably led to Christ by the Apostle himself. As a benefactor of the grace of God, Paul now is asking Philemon to extend their relationship to Philemon's former slave Onesimus. This case study of the interaction between Paul and Philemon could strongly resonate with any Asian American, especially in relation to a first- and second-generation discussion because of the similarities in the cultural dynamics.

The first dynamic that Paul appeals to with Philemon is the authority that he possesses as an apostle. He mentions in Phlm 8–9, "Accordingly, though I am bold enough in Christ to command you to do what is required, yet for love's sake I prefer to appeal to you—I, Paul, an old man and now a prisoner also for Christ Jesus." Paul obviously had apostolic authority and thus could potentially "command" Philemon if he wanted to do so. Philemon certainly knew and understood this. Paul then includes two other statements: 1) one of status as "an old man" verse 9a; and 2) one of need— "now a prisoner also for Christ Jesus." To refuse any of these requests culturally would be to shame Paul and to undermine his authority. Paul had position (as an Apostle), age (as an old man), and need (as a prisoner). How could Philemon refuse Paul to whom he himself was indebted for all that he had done? He could not! Similarly, these same appeals are often used in Asian American contexts by parents, bosses, and pastors as ways to "encourage" people to follow and submit to a request. This is often the way that interaction between these two parties would be done in the family, in business, or in a church setting. While the influence and motivation would be different in an Asian American context (probably from Confucianism), the outcomes of disobedience to this request would be the same (shame, lack of patronage) as the first-century dynamic. Younger Millennials, however, often resent this approach due to their entitlement issues and rebellion towards older authority figures. Younger people view this kind of directive as a forceful obligation in which they have no choice but to consent. Thus the term "voluntold" is used to describe this kind of interaction.

There were two additional passages in which Paul asserts his authority. Philemon 14 says, ". . . but I preferred to do nothing without your consent in order that your goodness might not be by compulsion but of your own accord." Also, Paul writes in Phlm 20, "Yes, brother, I want some benefit from you in the Lord. Refresh my heart in Christ." What is interesting in both these examples is that while Paul had every right culturally due to his position as an apostle to assert his authority, he chose to do otherwise. Paul is extending goodness and grace to Philemon through a relational appeal and partnership (Phlm 1, 9, 14, 17, 20). This approach would probably yield a better response of patronage from Philemon. In this passage, Paul acts as the patron, Philemon as the client, and Onesimus is the gift because he could then aid Paul through service. As a result, Onesimus's status is raised to being a fellow servant of the gospel (Phlm 13–14); a "beloved brother" (Phlm 16); and "a partner" (Phlm 17). DeSilva concludes that:

> Philemon really does appear to be in a corner in this letter—Paul has left him little room to refuse his request. If he is to keep his reputation for generosity and for acting nobly in his relations of reciprocity (the public reading of the letter creates a court of reputation that will make the evaluation), he can only respond to Paul's request in affirmation.[11]

While this episode may seem distant because it is a first-century occurrence, these kinds of practices consistently show up today in the twenty-first-century Asian American context. Similar to Paul's approach, there would be a mixture between authority directives as well as relational reciprocity. While immigrant first-generation people would be more directive, hierarchical, and authoritative in their approach, largely due to Confucian principles, more second-generation Asian Americans would utilize the mixed approach that Paul uses here in the book of Philemon. This mixed approach will be a much better way to relate to younger people rather than the "voluntold" approach. Again, this can apply to such scenarios as parents relating to children and especially to pastors requesting their congregants

11. DeSilva, *Honor*, 125.

to serve. This mixed approach will work well with Millennials (Generation Y) and Centennials (Generation Z) in working together in the future.

Other examples of Global Grace and its reciprocity can be found in the book of Romans. Paul describes the new life we have in Christ in Rom 6:12–13. Because of the new life we have, the proper response to God is obedience. In verse 13, Paul writes, "Do not present your members to sin as instruments for unrighteousness, but present yourselves to God as those who have been brought from death to life, and your members to God as instruments for righteousness." Another example of the reciprocity of Global Grace can be seen in Rom 8:12 where Paul uses debtor's language to describe the Christian life. Paul writes, "So then, brothers, we are debtors, not to the flesh, to live according to the flesh." We in a sense owe our entire lives to God because of the grace that he has bestowed upon us. In Rom 12:1, Paul writes, "I appeal to you therefore, brothers, by the mercies of God, to present your bodies as a living sacrifice, holy and acceptable to God, which is your spiritual worship." In this passage, Paul explains that since we have received salvation, his plea by the "mercies of God," should elicit a total worship to God by the presentation of our bodies in holy sacrifice. Thus, this gift is given to us and the reciprocation must be our bodies, as a living sacrifice and as part of our spiritual worship and service to him. These examples are just a small sampling of many different texts throughout Paul's letters (Gal 6:2; Eph 5:1–2; Phil 3:20–21; Col 3:1–2; 1 Thess 4:1; 2 Thess 2:13; 1 Tim 6:17; 2 Tim 2:22; Titus 2:11–14).

Examples of Global Grace

John Barclay, in his book *Paul and the Gift,* understood the different nuances of grace and explains these through what he calls "six (6) Perfections of grace." He explains that the term "perfection" is borrowed from the work of Kenneth Burke and "refers to the tendency to draw out a concept to its endpoint or extreme, whether for definitional clarity or for rhetorical or ideological advantage."[12] He further explains that, "Because of this complexity, there is no single form in which gift/grace is perfected, and no necessity that a perfection of one facet will entail a perfection of others."[13] As a result of this complexity, Barclay lists these six different categories for

12. Barclay, *Paul,* 67.
13. Ibid., 69.

grace that include superabundance, singularity, priority, incongruity, efficacy, and noncircularity.

For *superabundance,* this perfection of grace emphasizes the size, significance, and permanence of the gift. Barclay explains:

> . . . we are not concerned here with the content of the gift, which, in relation to God, may take many different forms. What is emphasized here is scale: the more excessive and more all-encompassing the gift, the more perfect it may appear.[14]

The next perfection is called *singularity,* in which the focus shifts from the gift itself to the giver, "specifically to the spirit in which the gift is given."[15] In this aspect, the singularity comes in that the giver's only mode in giving is to bestow goodness and benevolence to the receivers. The third perfection of grace is called *priority* in which the focus is now on "the timing of the gift, which is perfect in taking place always prior to the initiative of the recipient."[16] This type of grace focuses more on the manner of the giving. The fourth perfection is called *incongruity* that focuses on the choice of the recipient in being unconditional in giving to the recipient no matter of one's worthiness. The fifth perfection of grace is called *efficacy*. In this aspect of grace, the focus now shifts to the effect of the gift emphasizing more what has been achieved and then fulfilling what it was originally designed to accomplish. The sixth and final perfection of grace is called *noncircularity*. Barclay says, "A gift defined as gift by the fact that it escapes reciprocity, the system of exchange or *quid pro quo* that characterizes sale, reward, or loan? As we have seen, such is the modern notion of the 'pure gift.'"[17]

Barclay notes also that the nonreciprocal conception of grace was not very common in antiquity. Although not impossible within the culture, such a gift was certainly more foreign than it would be considered by today's standards.

While Barclay's different categories of grace may seem foreign to a Western understanding, they are helpful because of the parallels to the Eastern worldview. Jackson Wu has taken these six categories of perfection of grace and has presented a Chinese translation that parallels Barclay's terms. He shows *Superabundance* as (富足 / fù zú); *Singularity* as (自由 / zì yóu);

14. Ibid., 70.
15. Ibid., 70.
16. Ibid., 71.
17. Ibid., 74.

Priority (优先, perhaps 主动 / yōu xiān, perhaps zhǔ dòng); *Efficacy* (效力 / xiào lìbu); *Incongruity* (不赔得 or perhaps 不相称 / bú pèi dé or perhaps bù xiāng chèn); and *Noncircularity* (不互惠 / bù hù huì).[18] Wu also discusses and explains the Chinese dynamic of *guanxi* and notes that "Chinese intentionally use gifts to establish and enhance relationships."[19] These examples give further support of the global nature and depth of grace that goes far beyond the one-dimensional Western conception of grace.

Example of Western Grace

One of the most fascinating examples of the giving of grace has been the recent emergence of the New Reformed Movement and its focus on Gospel-centered preaching. This focus is promoted by groups such as the Gospel Coalition and modeled by pastors such as Timothy Keller and theologians such as D.A. Carson and John Piper. In essence, the message within this theological framework is that the gospel is news about what has been done by Jesus Christ on our behalf to put us right in our relationship with God. Keller writes:

> The gospel, then, is preeminently a report about the work of Christ on our behalf—that is why and how the gospel is salvation by grace. The gospel is news because it is about a salvation accomplished for us. It is news that creates a life of love, but the life of love is not itself the gospel.[20]

The appeal to this brand of theology for Asian Americans is significant because it is in contrast to the works-righteousness focus of typical Reformed theology that strongly parallels the Confucian work ethic within Asian culture. In other words, the emphasis on devotion over duty and on grace over works within Gospel-centered preaching brings a new and refreshing experience and perspective to Asian American Christians. Asian Americans who have been strongly influenced over their lifetime with an emphasis on duty even in regards to their religious service, often feel tired or even burned out. Thus, to hear, know, and subscribe to Gospel-centered preaching will seem like "the truth will set you free" (John 8:32).

---

18. Wu, *"Saved by Grace?"*
19. Wu, *"Saved by Grace?"*
20. Keller, *Center Church*, 31.

Gospel-centered preaching has had immense appeal to Asian American believers who have been steeped in a Reformed theological framework of works-righteousness. The duty and obligations of what these believers feel they ought to do have been a burden for so many in the Asian church. This is unfortunate, especially since the Scripture clearly states, "His commandments are not burdensome" (1 John 5:3). Somehow, whether it be through misunderstandings or not relying on the power of the Spirit of God, many Asian Americans have seen their relationship with God reduced to being just a religion of duty and good works. Thus, the emphasis on the Gospel has created freedom and provided a breath of fresh air to all who hear and respond to it.

There is a concern that comes with this new emphasis on grace with yet another ideology called the Free Grace movement made popular by preachers such as Tullian Tchividjian. This movement came from the Gospel-centered preaching focus but has carried it even further by suggesting that all is of grace, thus alleviating the need to do any works at all. Some have accused this movement of resembling antinomianism, that is a lawless type of living void of responsibility. In Rom 6:1–2 the Apostle Paul warned against this kind of living by those who would want to abuse grace by living lawlessly in order to allow grace to abound.

Conclusion

This chapter has given a cultural, historical, and biblical overview of the depth and breadth of the concept of grace. I used to think that Asian culture was completely devoid of grace. But now I realize that it was just a different type of grace, not the Western kind that I was used to knowing as an evangelical, Western Christian. Although grace is not a difficult concept to grasp, it has typically been oversimplified to the point that much of its beauty and power has been absent. The main aspects that have been missing have been the reciprocity and relationship intrinsic to this important concept and how it is necessary to see grace from several perspectives.

Our attempt to study the concept of grace using patronage as the bridge from first-century Greco-Roman ideology to twenty-first-century Asian American culture will provide a holistic and comprehensive picture that will offer many parallels and lessons for greater Christian living and testimony. Since history often repeats itself, both in the victories as well as the mistakes, the hope here is that the lessons of history and culture will provide a window of greater freedom, power, and growth for all Asian Americans for the glory and honor of God.

Due to the lack of understanding God's grace, Asian Americans are often faced with the dilemma of whether to serve in the immigrant church or to leave and to plant another church. The next chapter presents the advantages and disadvantages of both options.

Reflection Questions

1. Try to explain and differentiate Western Grace (WG) from Global Grace (GG) by giving contrasting principles of both.

2. What are some specific examples of Global Grace (GG) that you have seen in your own life, whether on the receiving or giving end of the situation?

3. In what ways does this new view of grace either bother you or resonate with you personally? Be specific.

4. Read Rom 11:6; Eph 2:7–10; and Titus 2:11–14 and reflect on how the grace of God has affected you. Write down a few examples of this from your life.

4

———

Should I Stay or Go?

Church Planting Versus the Immigrant Church

I REMEMBER UPON GRADUATION from seminary that nearly all of my Asian American classmates dreamed about planting a church. There were many reasons for this. Some were strong visionaries who wanted to create their own ministry with a unique emphasis or vision. Others dreamed about having a multiethnic or multicultural church for all people. But the biggest and most frequent reason that my classmates gave for planting a church was that they did not want to be part of an immigrant church. Specifically, they were tired of being under the leadership of first-generation Asian immigrants. Fast forward a few years and nearly all of these classmates did eventually plant a small, independent church. And unfortunately, after only three to five years, the church plants all folded. Many of these pastors no longer serve in pastoral roles but now have jobs in the marketplace.

What is the fascination with church planting? And why are so many Asian American pastors wanting to leave the immigrant church and all of its comforts in order to go to a more difficult and challenging situation in a church plant? The answer may be more related to negative implications about the immigrant church than to a strong, positive calling from God. Due to multiple hardships as well as ongoing misunderstandings, Asian American pastors are quick to leave the immigrant church and to go establish their own churches through church planting. While this may seem exciting and glamorous at first, it certainly brings many challenges as well. This chapter will highlight the advantages and challenges of church planting as well the issues involved in staying in an immigrant church.

Advantages of Church Planting

There are many wonderful aspects of doing a church plant. One of the first aspects is that it is simply new and exciting. When something new opens up in a city or community, people typically want to come and check it out. For this reason alone, many unchurched people or seekers are likely to attend a new church plant rather than go to an established, traditional church. Some aspects of an established church that are not so appealing to the unchurched may include the religious veneer that is associated with the different negative stereotypes of American Evangelicalism or some of the recent scandals and downfalls that have been highlighted in the media. Statistics also show that new church plants have the highest evangelistic conversion rate of all churches.

Perhaps the greatest benefit of a church plant, as well as the main reason that many pastors want to start a church plant within an Asian American context, is the desire to have more autonomy and freedom to make decisions related to vision, theology, and direction for their ministry. Many Asian American second-generation pastors typically have come from Duplex church models and they have always been under the leadership of the first generation. While there may be many advantages to the Duplex model, there are also many drawbacks. Aspects such as budgetary decisions or freedom to make decisions that are different from the first-generation church have not been an option for the English ministry. The second-generation church feels under the mercy and control of the first-generation church. Because of this, these pastors dream of one day having their own church and being able to make all of their own decisions.

Along with this autonomy comes the opportunity to create a new identity for the church. A church plant allows for a new, more refined vision that may be more progressive. This opportunity often spawns an independent church that has no affiliation with a mainline denomination. Thus, the church can be more missional in its approach and eclectic in its polity and theology. A church plant can have contemporary worship and meet in venues other than a traditional church building. This kind of church will have a stronger draw for Millennials than for the older generation. Millennials and unbelievers will not normally walk into a traditional church building or service, but they may be interested in a new church plant. This leads to the next big advantage of a church plant.

Church plants statistically and historically have been much more effective in bringing people to Christ than older, traditional churches. Some of the reasons for this include location and demographics, vision and relevance, distance and proximity, nontraditional approaches to church, multiethnic congregations, excitement, newness, freshness, and a focus specifically on evangelism. All of these factors are relevant ways to reach people in any given community. In terms of location, church plants can meet in local community centers, schools, hotels, or other nontraditional venues. Some churches have met in coffee shops or even in businesses. These nontraditional places are attractive to unchurched people because they are places that they would normally go to during the week. As a result, many different kinds of people of all ethnicities and social classes can potentially attend.

This leads to the next possible opportunity to break out of the mold of being an Asian church and turn into a multiethnic church. Many church planters are thrilled by the possibility to start a church plant with the intent of having non-Asians as a part of the ministry. So, they choose a name that is generic and all-inclusive to attract different ethnicities. They speak only English in the service (instead of the Asian language of the first generation). They may have a couple of non-Asians in the church who are placed into high profile roles such as the worship leader or the main greeter. The food after the service is served potluck style. All of these strategies are good attempts to be multiethnic. And while a new church plant may draw a few non-Asians and a few ethnically mixed couples, it will remain basically an Asian American church. The reason is that the leadership is most likely all Asian, the style of ministry is still Asian in some ways, and the majority of the people in the congregation are Asian. Dr. Sharon Kim, professor of sociology and Asian American studies, quotes Curtiss DeYoung in her book *A Faith of Our Own,* stating, "Scholars have defined a multiracial church as one in which no one racial group is 80 percent or more of the congregation."[1] If this is correct, then there really are fewer multiracial and multiethnic churches out there than claimed. Becoming a diverse and multiethnic church is simply not as easy as it seems. It is challenging mainly because the congregation members themselves may not be prepared for this or even for a church plant for that matter.

1. Kim, *Faith,* 156.

Disadvantages of Church Planting

One of the hardships that church planters face early on in the beginning stages of the church has to do with finances and funding. How do you pay for renting a location? How do you pay for the salaries of the pastor and staff? How do you do all the legal paperwork to become an independent, nonprofit organization? All of these are aspects of ministry that are not taught in seminary. And because all of their financial structures were already set up in the previous immigrant church situation, there was no need to learn any of this. The process becomes one of learning as you go. Another difficulty has to do with the independent status that many of these church plants desire. Independence implies there are no standard procedures, no consultants, and no precedents to follow.

Financially, it is very expensive to launch a church plant. Funds are needed to pay the rent, to pay the pastors, to print materials, and to cover many other hidden costs that are taken for granted when working within an immigrant church. While younger church planters typically avoid mainstream denominations, they are still open to working with church planting associations. This would include groups like the Acts 29 or Stadia Networks. The difference is that an association is broader theologically and denominationally, while a denomination normally functions only within its tradition, whether it be with Baptist, Presbyterian, etc. The main financial needs for a church plant are paying the rent and paying the pastor. For this reason, some associations are willing to give "seed" money in order to start a church plant. This money is given for a limited time, e.g., two years, until the church builds up enough momentum and congregational strength to be self-sustaining. A time frame of three to five years will give a good indication whether the church will survive and flourish or if it will just stop due to lack of growth or progress. Unfortunately, a high percentage of church plants close down around the five-year mark.

This leads to the biggest hurdle in church planting: the readiness of the congregants to take on all the responsibilities of ownership. Many church plants come out of already existing immigrant churches. Some of these church plants arise from amicable relations, but the majority of church plants are the result of a conflict and eventual split from an immigrant church. These situations are painful and even scarring. For this reason, some of the people who start these church plants have either a jaded perspective on ministry or some hurts that come from the previous church experience. This can lead to all kinds of problems. Here are a few of them.

First, it is always better to leave for a calling to something new, like a planned church plant, rather than being forced to start something out of default or negative circumstances. Hurt and pain can definitely affect a person's judgment and discernment. Leaving a church or going through a split is a very emotional experience that will require healing. This healing can happen either through professional counseling or just over time. Either way, the rawness of the hurt provides a poor foundation for starting something new like a church plant. Second, when people leave a bad situation, they are not always ready to step into a new role of greater responsibility and service. This kind of unhealthy foundation, does not bode well for starting a church.

Disadvantages of the Immigrant Church

For many people the thought of staying in an immigrant church seems like an unreasonable and untenable proposition. There are many reasons that young, English-speaking Asian American pastors decide to leave and go off on their own as previously noted. Despite the risk and all the hardships and challenges they will face, many younger pastors would love to take this risk. They feel stifled within an immigrant church. They feel restricted in terms of the vision, the outreach, and the opportunities to expand and evangelize. There seem to be many reasons to leave an immigrant church and to go and establish a new church plant.

One major challenge to staying within the immigrant church has to do with the leadership structure and the relationship between the two generations. Asian immigrant church leadership is typically hierarchical, autocratic, and singular in structure. This fits the first generation very well in light of the long history and the culture of both China and Korea with their many kings over the centuries. This singular leader is the head pastor who basically gives all the directives for the church. The irony of this style of leadership is that denominationally, these churches are usually Presbyterian, a denomination that calls for a plurality of elders or a board to lead the church. But even in historically Presbyterian churches, the personality of the one, dominant leader prevails.

In contrast, most second-generation pastors prefer the idea of working on a team with specifically gifted people serving within their strengths. This plurality of leadership can then provide important aspects such as accountability, teamwork, development, mentoring, and more availability from the staff. While this seems ideal for second-generation leaders, this is often looked down upon by the first generation. First, this kind of leadership structure is foreign to the history and culture of Asia. Second, the first-generation leaders often perceive the second-generation leaders to be lazy and not willing to work long and hard for the ministry. Long hours, hard work, and low pay are typically expected of the clergy because there is an underlying ideology that pastors need to suffer. This suffering mentality is meant to foster greater reliance upon the Lord, stronger faith and sanctification, and greater virtue and character for those who endure. It is important here to note that this kind of mentality is neither right or wrong. But rather, it is just a different mentality of different generations and cultures. This same understanding can and should be used for many of the potential differences and misunderstandings. An analogous example would be the difference between Eastern herbal medicine and Western medical treatments. Neither is better nor worse. Neither one is good nor bad. They are just different from one another.

Advantages of an Immigrant Church

There might be some people who would say that there are no advantages at all in being a part of an immigrant Asian church. But there actually are many advantages and even luxuries, as well as lessons to be learned by being a part of an Asian immigrant church. This last section concerning the lessons to be learned is probably the most beneficial of the three. If these lessons could be learned within the context of an immigrant church, then a pastor could be even more effective in the future as he leads a church plant.

Advantages and Luxuries

The advantages and luxuries of being in an immigrant church go hand in hand. It isn't until someone moves away from an immigrant church situation and starts a church plant, that he realizes all benefits the immigrant church provided. The first advantage of an immigrant church, that also brings all of its luxuries, is the use of a facility and all of the resources that come with it. The space of a church facility encompasses many facets, including the sanctuary, office space, parking, a baby room, and additional classrooms for Sunday School or Bible study. For English ministries, these resources are given free of cost. There is no rent to be paid, no charge for the water and power, and no mortgage to worry about. With the rising costs of property and renting, staying in an immigrant church saves a tremendous amount of money for the English ministry. Even the rent itself, for a smaller facility, can easily deplete the little money raised by a brand new church plant. All of the other expenses, including water, power, internet, furniture, copy machines, audio-visual equipment including sound systems, musical instruments, and projectors, can be quite expensive for a church plant that is just starting out. The costs and expenses add up quickly.

Another important value of being in an immigrant church is the opportunity to practice intergenerational ministry. The church, in this way, becomes a priceless venue in which the different generations of members can learn to live with and get along with each other. Titus 2:2–8 gives a biblical picture of how the different generations within a church can benefit from each other. Paul speaks about how the older men (Titus 2:2) can influence and mentor the younger men (Titus 2:6–7). In a similar way, the older women (Titus 2:3) can also teach and minister to the younger women (Titus 2:4–5). The lessons that are passed down in this passage focus more on character and virtue rather than in just doctrine or theology. Thus, much of what is taught in this passage may be through modeling and example. In other words, the younger men and women probably just observed the older believers and learned from them. The idea here is that the lessons of virtue were more "caught" than "taught." For the Asian American church, this kind of dynamic cannot occur unless there is an intergenerational mixture of men and women together on the same premises. Thus, the immigrant church is better positioned to do this than a church plant that consists of only younger people who are closer in age to one another.

This intergenerational opportunity also funnels down for the English speakers of the church to be able to teach, mentor, and influence young kids and children within the ministry as well. Since the younger generation will probably speak English as their first language due to being born in the States, it seems more likely that the second-generation English congregation would be the best group to mentor them. So now the Titus 2 principle applies again, but this time as the second-generation English speakers have the opportunity to teach and influence the younger Generation Z of students and children in the immigrant church. Again, this dynamic could occur in a church plant, but it is more likely to occur in an immigrant church.

Lessons Learned By Being in an Immigrant Church

There are a multitude of lessons that can be learned by just observing the older generation within an immigrant church. It must be noted here that the members of the first-generation immigrant church have had a very different experience than people who were born in the United States. The hardship of immigrating to the States, suffering financial struggles, and transitioning into a new culture without knowing the language, has created a very different disposition in this generation. They typically work hard and have a strong work ethic. They normally have much more endurance and perseverance because of all that they have gone through. They do not feel entitled but rather they value the opportunity to be in the United States. Their hardships have also led the first generation to a much more robust type of spirituality which includes disciplines such as prayer, giving, fasting, and sacrifice. These spiritual lessons in themselves can be very valuable for all generations to observe and embrace. The "faith of our fathers" could be one of the greatest lessons that could be passed down to the current generation of Asian American Christians.

In terms of the second-generation English pastor, there are numerous lessons from being in the immigrant church that could prove invaluable for the future of any minister. One of the first lessons is the ability to be humble, which will lead to a willingness to follow the church's leaders. Humility is taught in Confucianism as well as in Christianity. It is a universal virtue. Peter writes in 1 Pet 5:6, "Humble yourselves, therefore, under the mighty hand of God so that at the proper time he may exalt you." Peter also writes in 1 Pet 5:5, "God opposes the proud but gives grace to the humble." No matter the ethnicity or gender, all believers in Christ are to adorn themselves with this virtue of humility. The way that humility can be demonstrated is by the willingness of the second-generation English pastor to follow the lead pastor, the elders, and the older congregation. While this may certainly be a good thing, it is also most definitely not an easy thing for many. Paul again clarifies in Eph 5:18—6:8 that submitting to one another is a result of being filled with the Spirit. This is stated in Eph 5:21 where Paul writes, ". . . submitting to one another out of reverence for Christ."

In recent years, due to a number of situations and circumstances such as broken or dysfunctional families, there has been a rise in the number of younger people who have issues with authority. The way this is manifested is by rebelliousness, unwillingness to submit, outbursts of anger, and outright disobedience to authority figures. This is a problem not only for the older generation but also for the person who has this attitude because it carries over into other situations as well. This type of attitude can come out in a pastor's preaching, in staff relations, and in interaction with congregation members. Probably the best solution for this kind of problem is to get professional Christian counseling to seek healing. The inability to work with the other generation also leads many Asian Americans to leave the Asian church and to move to a Hotel model or to a megachurch for a period of healing.

Another important lesson to gain from the immigrant church has to do with leadership training. In an immigrant church, especially under a Duplex model, the decisions are typically made by the first generation and not by the English leadership. While this may seem terrible because the younger people are not included in the process, it actually reduces pressure because someone else is making the difficult decisions. In these situations, a younger pastor can watch and learn from both the good and the bad decisions, with little to no consequence on the English pastor's ministry. Leadership is not only learning what to do, a big part of leadership is also learning what not to do. Since the majority of the decisions of the church are made at the first-generation level, the bulk of the benefits or consequences fall on them. This is actually a pretty ideal circumstance.

The final personal lessons that a second-generation English pastor can learn in an immigrant church are endurance, contextualization, and conflict resolution skills. When it comes to endurance, second-generation English pastors do not have a good track record. They often don't stay longer than a couple of years in any given ministry and often try to "move up" into bigger and better churches or ministries. Longevity is not something that characterizes the second generation. Staying in an immigrant church, even when it is difficult, can build the character of the pastor so that he can know how to persevere. James 1:4 explains, "Let steadfastness have its full effect, that you may be perfect and complete, lacking in nothing." The context for this passage interestingly enough is within the contexts of trials (Jas 1:2). Hardship, or the crucible of suffering, can build or mold a person's character. Humility and endurance can be the result of suffering and hardship within an immigrant church.

Contextualization is yet another important skill that can apply cross-culturally as well as cross-generationally and even between believers and unbelievers. The Apostle Paul teaches on this in 1 Cor 9:19 when he says, ". . . for though I am free from all, I have made myself a servant to all, that

I might win more of them." Paul in this passage discusses how he is willing to be like others who are different from himself with the intent of winning them to Christ. In a similar manner, this same principle can apply to a "cultural win" by knowing, appreciating, and embracing the first-generation culture. Again, this skill is invaluable for anyone who desires to enter into ministry because ministry is about people. And the people we meet in ministry will be very diverse. They may be completely different from us, especially if they are unbelievers. The more we are able to relate with others, the more effective we will be in winning them over to Christ. The first-generation church is a different culture as well. Second-generation church members have a weekly opportunity to watch and learn important cross-cultural lessons from the first-generation church and to practice relating to them. The better this lesson can be learned in the present, the brighter the future will be for reaching a wider audience in the future.

By far, one of the best skills to learn within an immigrant church is that of conflict resolution. There will be conflicts in the church, either between different generations or even within the same generation. One of the best books to consult on this topic is Ken Sande's fine work, *The Peacemaker*.[2] In his book, Sande gives biblical and practical principles on how to resolve conflict. Oftentimes, rather than resolving conflict, people tend to avoid it. This results in an unspoken tension that builds up. When this happens, the problem becomes bigger than when it first began. The ability to discuss and solve problems, and even to forgive each other, becomes crucial in maintaining peace within a church.

The Scriptures give many important principles related to the issue of conflict. In Eph 4:26, Paul writes, "Be angry and do not sin; do not let the sun go down on your anger." The principle here is to resolve issues quickly and, hopefully, before the end of the day so that the anger doesn't fester and then turn into bitterness. In the next verse, Eph 4:27, Paul warns, ". . . and give no opportunity to the devil." Here Paul explains how an unresolved sin that festers in the heart can become a foothold for Satan to have influence over a believer. We are further instructed by Jesus that when dealing with sin or conflict, the parties should begin by speaking to each other in private (Matt 18:15). Finally, if it becomes too difficult to settle the issue, then others can be brought in to help mediate and arbitrate between the two parties (Phil 4:3). All of these are important principles and skills that are crucial to any pastor or leader, whether it be in an immigrant church or a church plant.

2. Sande, *Peacemaker*.

Conclusion

Church planting is important. New churches can impact society and the culture and can be an evangelistic force in any city. But the immigrant church also has an important place in the Kingdom of God, especially for first-generation immigrants who come to the United States wanting to find community and refuge. So how can these two strategies exist together, peacefully, and for the glory of God? Here are a few recommendations.

First, pastors who desire to someday plant a church would benefit greatly by staying in an immigrant church for several years prior to doing a plant. A pastor can learn the important values of humility, patience, submission, intergenerational ministry, contextualization, sacrifice, and conflict resolution. All of these lessons can best be learned in an immigrant church. Once there is a good sense of these values, then the pastor will be better prepared to go independent and start a new church. Without learning the important lessons listed above, the pastor will likely face many troubles and hardships ahead.

Second, large immigrant churches should be in the practice of preparing and sending out potential church plants for the future. This should be done with the full approval, support, and blessing of the mother church. Gifted leaders who can plant new churches should be chosen and trained for this mission. Families and individuals should be paired with the pastor for the future church plant so that the ministry can be viable and self-supporting. The immigrant church can then encourage the church plant by partnering with them spiritually and financially. This was the model of the local church seen clearly in the book of Acts. As the Gospel message went out from Jerusalem (Acts 1–8), to Judea and Samaria (Acts 9–13), and then to the outermost areas (Acts 14–28), the planting of local churches became a global movement. This kind of ministry can happen today as long as pastors and leaders are strategic, humble, and obedient to do the work of the King for the Kingdom of God.

Finally, the message of Jesus and the Gospel should always be a balance of truth and love (Eph 4:15). Jesus clearly states that a watching, unbelieving world will know that we are his disciples by our love (John 13:34–35). These are some of the important reasons why a good partnership in the Gospel (Phil 1:5) needs to be maintained even when churches separate. Even though Paul and Barnabas had conflict with each other leading to a separation (Acts 15:37–41), their decision actually doubled the efforts and ministry of the Gospel. May both the immigrant church and future church plants double the ministry of the Gospel for the glory of God!

Asian spirituality looks very different from the spirituality in the evangelical church at large because both are greatly influenced by culture. The next chapter describes a number of similarities and differences between Korean and Chinese expressions of spirituality arising from different characteristics of Korean and Chinese culture such as prayer, pastoral style, preaching style, etc.

Reflection Questions

1. Which advantages of either the Church Plant model or the immigrant church seem most appealing to you?

2. Which challenges of either the Church Plant model or the immigrant church scare you the most?

3. Which type of church, the church plant or the immigrant church, are you most passionate about and why?

4. Read Acts 13:1–3; Gal 2:11–14; and 1 Tim 3:15–16 and think of a few church plants that you are either a part of or aware of. Pray for them as they start so that they may continue to be effective for the cause of the Gospel.

5

Let's Get Spiritual

Comparing Korean and
Chinese Spirituality

THE LATE DALLAS WILLARD, in his book *Renovation of the Heart,* wrote, "Spiritual formation in Christ is the process by which one moves and is moved from self-worship to Christ-centered self-denial as a general condition of life in God's present and eternal kingdom."[1] As believers in Christ, spiritual growth and formation are essential parts of our Christian life. But it is also important to understand that there are not only different means to spiritual growth but also different expressions of it as well. For example, my wife Jen grows spiritually as she serves other people in the church. She is extremely gifted and kind in this ministry and she finds not only great satisfaction in serving but also spiritual renewal as well. For myself, however, reading a good book, hearing a lecture, or listening to a sermon is what sparks my growth in Christ. The expressions of spirituality are typically different from one person to another, especially as one examines the different Asian cultures. This chapter will focus on just two of these cultures and their expressions: Korean spirituality and Chinese spirituality.

A quick disclaimer must be stated here. First, it is important to note that quantifying and explaining spirituality is a difficult task in and of itself. The metrics for this are not very clear or tangible. It would be safe to say that descriptions of spirituality may be general tendencies more than specific descriptions. Second, it should be noted that the descriptions of both the Korean and the Chinese spirituality are broad generalizations. The descriptions may apply to a significant number of people, but there may be

1. Willard, *Renovation,* 77.

another large group that would deny any of these descriptions. This limitation is acknowledged and understood by the writer. Finally, in terms of the method of gathering data, much of what is described here came mainly through personal observations and from multiple interviews of people from various ages and backgrounds. The answers could vary based on region of the country, age of the person, gender, generation, or upbringing in the church. Again, these observations are general descriptions of tendencies viewed over a period of thirty years.

Commonalities Between Korean and Chinese Spirituality

Before looking at the differences between Korean and Chinese spirituality, it is important to note that there are many significant similarities or starting points as well. These similarities include: 1) a high view of God; 2) acknowledgement of the authority of Scripture; 3) high moral values and lifestyle; and 4) strong commitment to the local church. All of these values tie into many Asian values that are already intrinsically built into the two cultures. For example, a high view of God may also stem from the honorific submission of lower-status people to higher-status authority figures as taught in Confucianism.[2] Another example is the strong commitment of people to the local church, which is already primed by the influence of collectivist thinking as well as a filial piety[3] that leads to loyalty. These practices are normal in the two cultures and can easily be seen in the Asian mindset and worldview. Further aspects of each of these areas will be explored in the next sections.

High View of God

One of the strongest similarities between Korean and Chinese spirituality is their high view of God. There may be a number of reasons for this. Perhaps the main reason for this lies in the cultural and historical background of Confucianism and its influence. Specifically, the idea of a top-down authoritative structure may lead to the respect and honor given to God as Father. This perspective sees God as someone who needs to be revered, honored, and obeyed at every level. The transference of this kind of honor

2. Chapter 9 discusses Confucianism and its influence on Asian culture.
3. Filial piety will be discussed more in chapter 9.

is seen all throughout Confucianism and the five types of relationships that are key to its ideology as well as in the different human relationships in both Korean and Chinese religious practices. This same honor and authority is also given to pastors, elders, adults, parents, and certainly to God, the highest-ranking authority possible.

Authority of Scripture

In addition to God the Father being honored and revered, the written source of the Holy Scriptures also plays a major part in guiding and directing the spirituality of Korean and Chinese spiritual practices. The Bible, the Word of God, is basically God's directive and voice to the believer for everything related to life and godliness. Without a clear understanding of the Word of God, a Christian would not know God's will or desires. For this reason, Bible studies have always been an important part of the religious life of Korean and Chinese believers. Bible studies might meet on a Wednesday night, a Friday night, a Saturday early morning, and on Sunday, either before or after the service. The Bible study is normally a consistent part of the believer's life from youth group all the way through adulthood. Without Bible study many believers would feel incomplete or not "fed" spiritually.

For some, this high view of God's Word is directly linked to the previous idea of a high view of God himself. While God is the authority, his Word is the authoritative directive or command that must be obeyed. For people who have functioned in a hierarchical[4] culture or system, to obey a command or word is the easiest and best way to function. People in a hierarchical society are good at following and are used to doing so without question. The Bible and God are both viewed as higher authorities that must be followed at all costs.

High Moral Values

Virtue and honor in an Asian worldview go hand in hand. A person who is virtuous in character is highly respected and honored. On the other hand, a person who is immoral and not virtuous is seen as shameful and as an embarrassment to the society. To not be in accordance to a high moral code violates the honor/shame dynamic of Asian culture; it also deviates from

---

4. Chapter 7 will discuss the hierarchical nature of Asian culture in more detail.

the collectivist practice of community. Following this kind of thinking, being different challenges the norm.

In many ways, the Asian standard of morality resembles Western morality from societal standards of past decades. Issues such as drinking, smoking, divorce, premarital sex, profanity, disobedience to parents, gambling, pornography, and lying are strongly frowned upon due to this strong moral standard. In this regard, the Asian church is somewhat "behind" the decline of Western societal morality. While some think that this is "old-fashioned," others believe that this is a good thing because of the innocence and protection modeled, especially to the youth of the church.

This characterization doesn't mean that Asians are exempt from these kinds of practices. It just means that these practices may be happening more in a covert manner due to the possible shame it would bring to the individual as well as to the family. The honor aspect of Asian culture, along with the collectivist group dynamic, can work together to provide accountability to a person in either the Korean or the Chinese communities. As a result, many gatherings occur at church or at a church member's home. Alcohol or other questionable items may be hidden at these gatherings and would certainly be absent if the pastor is present. Some have suggested that these high moral standards may resemble legalism in differing degrees. This is an ongoing debate that usually results in differing opinions based on one's generational origin.

Strong Commitment to the Local Church

Asian Americans have long been known to gather together regularly and enjoy community. This is due in part to the collectivist-communal mindset[5] that is part of the Asian worldview. The focus on "we" versus "I" is best seen within the context of the local church. Gathering on Sundays is just a small part of this characteristic for Asian Americans. Asian Americans also gather for midweek worship on Wednesdays, Bible studies on Friday or Saturday night, and small groups on any other available night. Many of these gatherings also consist of a full meal for all to join in as part of the fellowship. For some Asian Americans, typically of the older, more traditional generation, to miss church on Sunday would almost be considered a "sin" of sorts in their thinking.

---

5. See chapter 7 for more information about the communal nature of Asian culture.

It is important to note that generationally, this dynamic is beginning to change. For example, a typical first-generation churchgoer would never want to miss church for any reason other than sickness. This habit has continued for those who were born from the 1960s through the 1980s. However, Millennials in particular have a more relaxed view of commitment to church attendance. This is seen most clearly in the frequent vacations younger people take, as well as in their children's involvement in sports that often overlap with Sunday services.

When it comes to vacations, as well as to children's sports involvement, there seems to be a pendulum swing of generations regarding parents and their children. Part of this swing may be a feeling of the current parents being deprived of opportunities when they were children. The change may be due to financial hardship faced by the older generation or more so due to the previous generations' high religious commitment to the local church. These older parents from the previous generation would never miss church and would sometimes even force their children to attend Sunday school whether the children liked it or not. This may have created some animosity that would later show up in the next generation's views of the church. This in turn has led to a shift to the other extreme where today's parents may opt for a vacation or for a child's sports opportunity over going to church. This appears to be in large part a reactionary shift from the previous generation.

For pastors of Asian American churches, there are a number of concerns that come with this shift. First, church members are missing frequently and consistently from the congregation. This is especially problematic for those who serve in the church (i.e., Sunday school teachers, ushers, worship leaders, etc.). Secondly, unless these families attend another worship service, like a Saturday night service, then they miss out on community worship for the week. Finally, and most importantly, the message that is implicitly communicated by these younger parents to their children is that church is simply not a priority. The consequences for this message may be very damaging and detrimental for future generations.

Differences Between Korean and Chinese Spirituality

Despite the shared cultural features of the Korean and Chinese church, there are some distinct characteristics to each one. We will examine these differences in the following section.

Korean Spirituality

One of the most significant markers of Korean Christians is their different expressions and practices of spirituality. Some of these practices include daily early morning prayer, fasting, and sharing food with each other. The Korean people have been known for having a deep heritage of spirituality that characterizes their Christianity. The focus of this examination will include the influences and expressions that characterize Korean spirituality.

Influences

Much of Korean spirituality comes from Buddhist and Confucian influences.[6] As a result, the religion and spirituality is syncretistic in essence. What this means is that while the practices and expressions may have begun from either Buddhist and Confucian roots, the attached meaning and significance has shifted towards new Protestant Christian beliefs. Examples of this are also found in the West with such holidays as Easter or Christmas that originally had pagan roots but were later celebrated by Christians with new meanings.

Expressions

Korean spirituality has been described as passionate, emotional, loud, long, expressive, mystical, and fervent. While there may be several different practices of Korean spirituality, this section will focus on just two specific expressions: daily morning/dawn prayer and fervent prayer or *sae-baek ki-do*. Morning prayer has long been an anchoring characteristic of Korean spirituality. At the break of dawn, hundreds and thousands of people gather from far and wide to worship at 5:00 A.M. Korean Christians wake up extra early and come before work to meet the Lord and to worship together with their church. Mark 1:35 is often quoted as a verse where Jesus did the same. It reads, "And rising very early in the morning, while it was still dark, he departed and went out to a desolate place, and there he prayed." These early morning prayer services not only occur throughout the year, but also during special extended periods of thirty to forty days of consecutive prayer services which are offered for the entire church to come pray for a specific

6. See more about Buddhist and Confucian influences on Asian culture in chapters 8 and 9.

cause. Oftentimes, these early morning gatherings are held at the beginning of the year to rally around a theme for the whole church. This aspect of spirituality is a unique part of the Korean culture that is influenced by the Buddhist practice of meeting the gods in the early morning with the intent of appeasing them. This Christian form of morning prayer is considered by many to be one of the strongest points of Korean spirituality due to the high level of commitment to this important spiritual practice.

Another well-practiced part of Korean spirituality is a type of prayer called *tong-sung-ki-do,* which translates as "same prayer."[7] This type of prayer is typically done by whole groups or congregations simultaneously. *Tong-sung-ki-do* is often done during the morning prayer time. It is a time when everyone in the congregation prays simultaneously. The prayer is loud, long, emotional, and passionate. A large portion of this prayer is devoted to crying out in repentance to the Lord. Similar practices can be found in Scripture passages such as Judges 10:10, "And the people of Israel cried out to the Lord saying, 'We have sinned against you, because we have forsaken our God and have served the Baals.'" This time of prayer is also a time of emotional release when typically quiet and reserved people can be open, vulnerable, and expressive to what they are feeling. Much of the content of this kind of prayer is geared towards repentance and supplication before the Lord.

It is important to clarify here that although this time of *tong-sung-ki-do* may look like a time of speaking in tongues, that may not necessarily be the case. While the charismatic practice of tongues does happen during this time, more often than not, the people are just praying expressively in their own Korean language. They have been heard crying out, "Lord, Lord, have mercy" (*Joo-yo, Joo-yo*) as part of their prayer. Part of this request is to be able to approach God, the Honorable One, by requesting for the unworthy one (the person praying) to be able to ask God for strength and cleansing. People continue by praying for health, the church, missions, prosperity, safety, well-being, and for family members.

What are the motivations for Korean Christian spirituality, especially in America? Pak et al. explain in the introduction to their book *Singing the Lord's Song in a New Land* what role these practices may play in the culture:

> For Korean American Christians, practicing their faith gives structure to the chaos caused by many generations of turmoil on Korean soil, and by the efforts of immigration to the United States,

7. Pak et al., *Singing,* 36.

such as cultural, political, and economic discontinuities; discrimi-
nations; and generational conflicts. Practicing faith gives meaning
in the midst of apparent meaninglessness.[8]

This spiritual dynamic maintains a tradition of community for Koreans
who are now experiencing the newness of a foreign land. The spiritual
practice also reinforces the cultural dynamic of the collectivist mindset as
they unite to worship God.

Chinese Spirituality

While Chinese spirituality shares some similarities with Korean spirituality,
there are some notable differences. Some would describe Chinese spirituality as being very cognitive, sober, reserved, moral, pragmatic, and unified.
The next section will examine the influences, expressions, and motivations
that characterize Chinese spirituality.

Influences

Chinese spirituality also has Buddhist and Confucian influences just as
Korean spirituality does. But added to this are the influences of Taoism and
superstition as well. Taoism values a harmony with the universe that often
becomes an unwillingness to engage in confrontation of any kind. This focus on avoiding conflict can lead to withdrawal, passive aggressiveness, and
even a false sense of harmony. Harmony and peace are strong values in the
Chinese culture. Thus, when a person is in conflict with another person,
they will typically avoid the situation and, in some cases, if the problem
continues, they will leave the church.

Another facet of the Confucian influence on the Chinese American
church has to do with a strong emphasis on filial piety.[9] This value has
caused the unconscious creation of an inner circle consisting of blood-
related family members as well as long-standing members who have known
each other in some cases since the beginning of the church. The strong
point of this filial piety is that there is strong loyalty and commitment to
one another because of the family relationship and the shared history in
the church. The downside is that it then creates an inside group versus an

8. Ibid., xiii–xiv.

9. Chapter 9 presents more details about the influence of filial piety on Asian culture.

outside group of either newcomers or people who are not related to anyone in the church. For these outsiders, it is very difficult, if not impossible, to break into the inner circle.

Expressions

Probably the main feature of Chinese spirituality is its emphasis on the mind and on knowledge that leads to moral excellence. The main difference between Korean and Chinese spirituality has to do with how each culture processes truth. Specifically, this distinction will be demonstrated by preaching styles and the way people process the teaching. Again, these are general stereotypes that may apply to a majority of people but not to all people. There can certainly be exceptions to these generalizations. For Korean Americans, truth is best processed through an emotive grid. As a result, Korean sermons would be mostly narrative stories, anecdotal, with different emotional degrees of humor, sadness, and joy. For this reason, pastors such as Francis Chan, would be a huge favorite among Korean Americans. He embodies the best of storytelling in and through his sermons.

For Chinese Americans, however, the processing grid for truth is the mind, and sermons are processed through a cognitive dimension. Thus, the best kinds of sermon are very organized, systematic, and linear. One of the best examples of this kind of speaker is John MacArthur, who typically speaks in a verse-by-verse, expositional preaching of the passage. His messages are very logical and heady, and the primary goal is to explain the truth of the passage. One of the biggest ironies behind this comparison is that Francis Chan is Chinese, yet he preaches more in an emotive style that is more fitting for Korean Americans!

It is interesting to note that Samuel Ling, in his book *The "Chinese" Way of Doing Things*, makes a distinction in the style of preaching based more on generations rather than on ethnicities. He writes:

> The goal of preaching, according to this "Chinese model," is to exhort the congregation to lead moral lives, to develop character, and to "grow spiritually." Stories are used all throughout the sermon. The tone is mostly authoritative, but sometimes paternalistic. The sermon grows out of the life experience and ministry experience of the preacher. It is light on expository and doctrinal content, but

heavy on heart-felt response to the challenge of living the Christ life in real-life situations.[10]

Ling does later acknowledge that younger pastors, both in the OBC and ABC generation, utilize an expository style of preaching. He is hesitant to label this kind of preaching as a Western model because even some younger Chinese scholars in the Chinese Church preach in this manner. He establishes that this type of preaching resembles, in form at least, "the contemporary popular magazine article."[11] Further, he characterizes this form by stating, "There is biblical (and sometimes doctrinal) content; and the content is aimed at behavioral change through application and illustrations."[12] He does also acknowledge that "the strength of this kind of preaching is that it is aimed at helping Christians answer certain questions about the Bible, and to live Christian lives in the contemporary world."[13]

So, why is it important to be aware of this characteristic when it comes to the church and choosing pastors? In selecting a lead pastor for a church, it will be extremely important in matching the right kind of spirituality with the congregation. In my experience, I've seen many mismatches in pairing pastors with congregations. For example, if Chinese congregations, which tend to be very cognitive, hire a Korean pastor, who most likely is an emotive preacher, then the congregations end up being disappointed. On the flip side, the same is true when a Korean congregation, which tends to be emotive, hires a cognitive Chinese pastor, there is also a misalignment. These differences are very important factors to consider when matching the general type of spirituality of the people so that a congregation will grow spiritually.

Theology, Morality, and Education

Now that we have seen the different preferences of preaching styles between Korean and Chinese believers, we will explore how the two groups handle the matters of theology, morality, and value of education. Regarding theology, Chinese Christians, tend to be more cognitive and will value sound, logical, and systematic theology more than Koreans. This preference,

10. Ling, "Chinese" Way, 163–64.
11. Ibid., 165.
12. Ibid., 165.
13. Ibid., 165.

coupled with the strong weight of morality, is demonstrated by the importance of teaching the Bible in the Sunday School. The rationale behind this
is that good theology will lead to solid morality. And the place for all of
this to happen is the sphere of the Bible studies and time spent in Sunday
School. For this reason, the focus on quality Christian education in the
Chinese church will manifest itself in the finances and resources applied to
the different departments related to Christian education. This money will
be utilized for curriculum, retreats and rallies, Vacation Bible school, and
hiring competent youth pastors who will preach and teach the Bible well.

For Korean churches, experience seems to be valued more than
the propositional theology that is taught. Theology is important, but the
experiential is emphasized more frequently. Theologically, for example,
charismatic practices of speaking in tongues, giving prophecies or words of
discernment, and miracles have been seen all throughout Korean churches,
even across denominations. This is certainly unusual, especially since many
Korean churches are from the Reformed or Presbyterian denominations
that historically have held to a cessationist understanding of the sign gifts.
This emotional disposition of Korean culture and the expressive worship fit
well with the Charismatic practices and theology.

Pastors and Ministry

The perspectives of Korean and Chinese cultures toward pastors in ministry are vastly different. These differences also include how and why Korean
and Chinese people will follow their leaders. In Korean culture, pastors are
highly esteemed and respected. Part of the reason for this is due to the
thought that pastors are called and "anointed" by the Lord for this special
and high calling. While this may be partially true, this view may be difficult
to defend and support biblically. Much of the respect that is given to many
pastors may be due to the honorific nature of Confucianism. The pastor is
seen as an authority figure and as a servant of the Lord. In some cases, this
kind of respect has been taken too far in that some pastors are lavishly provided with excessive resources. Another cultural factor is that these Korean
pastors are given the freedom to make autocratic decisions independent
of anyone else. In this way the pastor/leader is never questioned or challenged for any of his decisions. While this may seem favorable for a pas-
tor/leader, it can be a dangerous situation because he lacks accountability.
As a result, congregations unquestionably follow their leaders, sometime

blindly, no matter the direction that the leader may go either theologically or philosophically.

The Chinese pastor is a very different case. While the Korean culture holds the pastor in very high esteem, the Chinese culture often sees the pastor as someone who has failed to succeed in a "real job." In other words, the pastor's role is seen as a default to other vocations such as being a medical doctor, a lawyer, or an engineer. According to this perspective, the pastor is likened to a beggar who is dependent on the congregation for financial support. For this reason, the pastor is not as highly esteemed nor seen as having the same kind of divine appointment as in the Korean church.

One of the most interesting parts of a Chinese pastor's calling is that he is typically encouraged to pursue another vocation first before going into full-time ministry. As a seminary professor, I have witnessed this personally. A number of our Chinese students have full-time careers as doctors, engineers, and lawyers and begin seminary as a second career because they desire to serve in full-time ministry. When asked how and why they took this longer route, the answer is typically the same. They promised their parents to get a "real job" first before taking on the "beggar's" career of being a pastor. This journey is certainly honorable, but also very long, averaging several years to a decade for completion. A possible role model or influence for this whole journey may be the missionary Hudson Taylor. Taylor was a British missionary who went to China and founded the China Inland Mission near the end of the nineteenth century. His ministry and impact birthed thousands of conversions and hundreds of missionaries in China. He acculturated himself by dressing in Chinese clothing, learning the language, and adopting the culture. But prior to being a missionary, he went to medical school and was a doctor. Many Chinese believers revere Hudson Taylor and often want their children to follow in his footsteps.

Due to the Chinese Christians' strong stress on doctrine and theological principles, they are not so apt to follow a leader as quickly and easily as Koreans. They would initially challenge the leader rather than follow his lead. Much of this stems from the view Chinese people have of their pastor. They respect him to a degree but would not necessarily see him as an "anointed one" who is chosen by God to do his work. This may seem like an extreme opposite to Korean people's response to pastors, but it could actually be a healthy way of holding the pastor/leader accountable. It will also force the pastor to be well prepared and studied in order to move forward with any decisions and it will require the congregation to know the Bible well enough to challenge or to correct the pastor if necessary. Consistent accountability is always a good practice.

Praise and Worship

A very interesting part of the whole diversity of spiritual expression is best seen through the differences in praise and worship between Korean and Chinese congregations. Even though the music, lyrics, and notes may be the same for the worship songs, the tempo, beat, and the way that the music is played can be quite different. One way to explain this may be that Chinese worship leaders play the notes accurately and correctly. They play the music well and on tempo. But that is it. Korean worship leaders, on the other hand, play the notes of course, but may play it with more emotion and feel. This should not be surprising in light of the earlier discussion that generally speaking Koreans may be more emotive while Chinese may generally be more cognitive. Again, they play all the "right" notes, but the music doesn't have the extra unction that may be found with Korean worship leaders.

An example of this was seen at a large gathering for Asian American church leaders. There were many different kinds of Asian Americans present including Chinese, Japanese, Korean, Vietnamese, Indonesian, and more. The worship band for this event was quite large, consisting of twelve people. While the songs were correctly played, it was played in a very straightforward way. As a result, the audience stood but did not express themselves with passion, clapping of hands, crying, or raising of hands. And although the band was fairly sizeable, the music was not very moving or emotive. The next day, the suggestion was made to add another musician, a bassist, who happened to be Korean, to the band. In a band structure, the bassist carries the rhythm and can add much to the tempo and rhythm of the songs. When he played, the band was significantly different. The music was faster, more upbeat, and definitely more emotive. The audience responded by clapping their hands, moving their bodies, raising their hands, and passionately crying out to the Lord. The worship set strongly resembled a Korean worship setting because of the addition of this one Korean bassist. This example points to the emotive disposition of Korean culture expressed through praise.

Buildings and Money

Another very different approach for Korean and Chinese churches has to do with money in general and the expression of this through buildings specifically. It might be said that when it comes to spending money, Korean Christians may be fairly generous, while Chinese Christians are very frugal. Another way of stating this is that Koreans may be excessive in their spending, while Chinese people may be almost stingy. This is most clearly shown in the different church buildings of each culture. Koreans are typically influenced religiously by the example of Buddhist temples, which are very beautiful and aesthetically pleasant. Part of the reason for the aesthetics of the Buddhist temple is to appease the gods. Korean churches also tend to be ornate. Some of the features in a Korean church may include a large cross, marble floors, stained glass windows, fountains, statues, large lobbies, brightly lit sanctuaries with the latest innovations in technology, including large video screens. The latest, best, high-tech equipment are considered necessary in order to enhance the worship. All of these features are lavishly designed and wonderfully spread throughout the church campus.

In contrast, for many Chinese churches, the values and goals are to be practical, functional, plain, and frugal. The ambiance of the church is very different from a Korean church. There are no marble floors, fountains, statues, or stained glass windows. Instead, there are very plain walls. The signage and structures are fairly old, not having been changed or upgraded for many years. The sanctuary has older equipment and no state-of-the-art technology. But as long as it works and as long as it carries out its intended function, everything is well. The plainness of everything in the church is not because there are no funds available. It is simply a more modest approach that saves the money and only spends when necessary, whether it be for missions, a mercy ministry, or special occasions.

Resolving Conflict

No matter the ethnicity, culture, or church, all people have conflicts with each other. Korean and Chinese Christians have both succumbed more to their cultural dispositions in solving conflict than to the biblical instructions on this subject. The two negative extremes to conflict have been either an avoidance response (more characteristic of Chinese) or an attack response (often characteristic of Koreans). Both are negative and neither lead to resolution. Jesus, however, tells us in Matt 5:9, "Blessed are the peacemakers, for they shall be called sons of God." Paul exhorts believers in Rom 14:19, "So then let us pursue what makes for peace and for mutual edification." Finally, Paul writes in Eph 4:32, "Be kind to one another, tenderhearted, forgiving one another, as God in Christ forgave you." These timeless principles, along with the application of the Gospel can serve as a powerful testimony to a watching world that is often skeptical of the church.

Oftentimes, church conflicts are personal, sometimes generational. What are ways to help alleviate the tension and the conflict? One way to resolve conflicts between the two congregations is to have mediators who speak both English and the mother language. I often refer to these kinds of people as "bridgers" since they basically help bridge the gap, especially in times of conflict. In their negotiation and mediation, the goal should be to help each side to understand the other. These conflicts are difficult to overcome because they often happen over a long period of time. But with a lot of prayer, wise counsel and patience, and wise people to help resolve the issues, resolution can be accomplished.

Conclusion

This chapter has attempted to describe the similarities and differences between Korean and Chinese spirituality. Although we have made huge generalizations, the hope is that they become a clue and a small window so that pastors and leaders will know how best to encourage and assist different believers to grow spiritually in their faith. More study and detail can certainly be done to go deeper on this subject and, I trust, there will be follow-up writings and lessons developed to help foster a healthy spiritual environment for all churches no matter the ethnicity.

In the next section we examine in depth the sources of the cultural complexities that arise between Asian and American cultures. A major difference is in the definition of a person. We begin by presenting some thoughts on the image of God in order to understand how the different definition of a person can lead to different ways to reflect God more clearly.

Reflection Questions

1. Which traits of Korean spirituality or Chinese spirituality do you best identity with?

2. What do you think causes these groups to differ in their spirituality?

3. Which trait within each type of spirituality do you feel is the most helpful for you? Why?

4. Reflect in prayer on Ps 103:12; Rom 6:1; 8:1; and Eph 2:8–9 and write what God is speaking to you about as a result of reflecting on these issues.

SECTION 2

Understanding the Cultural Complexities in Asian American Life and Ministry

S ECTION TWO EXPLORES THE Asian and American cultural complexities that work against grace. A major difference between the Asian and American cultures is the definition of the person. In American culture the person is an autonomous individual, while in Asian culture the person is part of a family or community. In order to better understand the two perspectives, Sheryl begins this section with an explanation of the concept of being made in the image of God (chapter 6).

In chapter 7 Sheryl uses a theory of culture to clarify differences between American and Asian cultures. The chapter explains that people live by either a strong or a weak view of the degree to which people are different (Structure) or the same (Community). The American culture is described as having a Weak Structure and Weak Community, as opposed to Asian culture, which has Strong Structure and Strong Community.

Chapter 8 further discusses the difference between the two cultural types. It shows how American dichotomistic thinking reflects an Individualistic definition of the person, while Asian holistic thinking reflects a collective definition of the person. The two definitions shape different perspectives that are reinforced by language. In chapter 9 Sheryl explores how Confucian relational roles reinforce the Strong Structure of hierarchical Asian culture. Chapter 10 explains how Buddhist and Taoist thinking reinforce Strong Community through Asian reciprocal practices.

6

We are All Made in God's Image[1]

THE PREVIOUS CHAPTERS HAVE presented various scenarios that reveal how both the Asian and the American culture create complexities in Asian American life and ministry and how both cultures can misinterpret Scripture. We have also seen how aspects of Asian culture are similar to first-century culture and provide insights into God's grace. We have looked at ways that culture distorts what God intended. In order to untangle the cultural complexities that prevent people from experiencing God's grace, we next need to consider whether we have a cultural or a biblical view of who we are—people made in God's image. If we understand who we are as created in God's image, we can also accept others in the same way that God accepts us, as made in his image. If we have a cultural view of who we are, we may be unable to accept not only ourselves but also others as being made in God's image.

This chapter provides the biblical basis for thinking and acting in light of what it means to be created in God's image. Being made in God's image means we are each a beloved person for who we are, not for what we do. Being created in God's image means that there is something about us that God considers good (Gen 1:31). God intended this goodness to be reflected in our everyday actions that are based on what Christ has done for us. When we rely on God's will that is based on God's truth and we are guided by the Holy Spirit, the fruit of the Spirit abounds in our lives, and the body of Christ functions harmoniously. We are also able to understand and accept God's grace given to us through Christ's actions on the cross through our devotion to God demonstrated by our grace-filled actions with others.

---

1. For more information about the image of God see Silzer, *Biblical Multicultural Teams*, 9–19.

We are Created in the Image of God

If we do not believe or cannot accept that we are unconditionally loved by God because we are made in the image of God and that God loves us for who we are and not for what we do, it will be difficult for us to accept others or to relate well to others. We will also have difficulty accepting different cultural behaviors if we do not believe that we and others are all created in the image of God. Unfortunately, all cultures promote many different false beliefs about who we are. We have each been socialized to unconsciously think and believe that we are worthwhile only if we live up to our respective cultural standards rather than because God loves us unconditionally because he created us in his image.

When we are in the midst of life or ministry challenges, we do not often think about who God intended us to be. We often think of the wrongs that other people have committed against us, and, if we are honest, the negative feelings or behavior we have towards them. Although we recognize that these are not the feelings or behavior God intended, we somehow feel justified in our actions because we believe our way is biblical and, therefore, the other way of doing things must be wrong and not biblical.

In order to understand our response to challenges, we first need to understand who we are as God intended us to be as created in his image. Once we can accept ourselves as God intended, it is easier for us to accept others. When we understand how much we ourselves are in need of Christ's redemptive work on the cross, we can embrace others as similarly in need of God's love. This understanding will also open our minds to how holding on to our different ways of doing things can prevent us from reflecting God's image. All human cultures have both positive and negative elements, reflecting God's image in some ways and fostering false beliefs in other ways.

From the beginning, God recognized diversity in creation. The diversity of languages seen in Gen 10 was temporarily blocked when people tried to be like God, imposed a single language, and built a tower to make a name for themselves (Gen 11).[2] God's desire was to unite diverse people from every language and culture through the person and work of Christ. This complete unity will take place in heaven around the throne when people from every nation, language, and tribe will praise and worship God

2. Smith, *Gift of the Stranger*, 7–8.

together (Rev 5:7; 7:9). However, God also desires that we experience this unity now (Eph 4:3).

In order to move towards the unity that God desires, we each need to understand who God is, what it means to be made in the image of God, how the image of God works, and how sin can distort the image of God. We will look at each of these topics in the following sections.

Who is God?

We are not fully able to understand who God is this side of heaven. However, Scripture gives countless descriptions of who God is and how God acts. He is the Creator of the world and everything in it (Gen 1). God not only created the world, but also keeps the world and the people in it alive (Acts 17:28; Col 1:16–17). Our very existence is only possible through God the Creator, who sustains the life that was first breathed into Adam (Gen 2:7).

As Creator, God is all-powerful, and nothing is impossible for him (Luke 1:37). God's wisdom and knowledge are much greater than any human wisdom and knowledge (Rom 11:33), and God's foolishness is wiser than human wisdom (1 Cor 1:25). What we consider righteous is just filthy rags to God (Isa 64:6).

God is also holy (Ps 99:9), righteous (Dan 9:7), and just (2 Thess 1:6). He is light and life (John 1:4), and there is no evil in him (Ps 92:15). God is like no one else. He not only created us, he also loves us so much that he sent his Son to die for our sins and provide a means of salvation for us (John 3:16) so that we can be conformed to Christ's image (Rom 8:29).

God is also described as our Father who takes responsibility for us as his children (Isa 64:8; 2 Cor 6:18). As a human father makes decisions for the care of his children, so God takes care of us. He takes responsibility for us and desires to be our authority figure and decision-maker. We can also know God by knowing Christ—the word, the truth, and the way (John 1:1; 14:6). Christ set the example for us through his obedience. He became a human being so that he could die for our sins (Phil 2:5–11). Christ lived the Truth in his earthly life and, as such, set an example for us to do the same. God the Holy Spirit guides us and teaches us the things we need to say and do (Luke 12:12; John 14:26; 1 Cor 2:13). The Spirit can guide our behavior and enable us to demonstrate the fruit of the Spirit—love, joy, peace, patience, kindness, goodness, faithfulness, gentleness, and self-control (Gal 5:22–23)—in our interpersonal relationships.

Three Views of the Image of God

There are basically three main views of what it means to be made in the image of God—the substantive, the functional, and the relational.[3] These three views reveal the characteristics of God: 1) as authority (2 Cor 6:18), responsible for decision-making (e.g., giving the Law); 2) as responsible for creation (Col 1:16) and truth (John 14:6); and 3) as responsible for community (1 Cor 12:13). When we reflect the image of God in these three ways, God, rather than we, receives the glory. We are also able to love others as God loves us.

The substantive view of the image of God sees the image of God as a basic characteristic of human nature, in particular our human will (i.e., the ability to make choices or decisions). The functional view of the image of God relates to how humans fulfill God's command to take responsibility for creation. The relational view of the image of God focuses on how humans reflect God through relationships with God, with our fellow humans, and with God's creation. These three views are explained in the next sections.

Substantive View—Choosing to Depend on God

The substantive view of the image of God views the image of God as something very basic to people; that is, something that uniquely distinguishes people from the rest of creation—the freedom of choice or the will. Humans are different from the rest of creation.[4] God created us with the ability to be like him by being able to choose between good and evil (Gen 3:5). Just as Adam and Eve had the opportunity to choose to follow God's commands or to disobey them, we also have the ability to choose to obey or disobey God's commands. Through our will we choose whether to depend on God or to rely on our own wisdom or knowledge (Prov 3:5–6).

James (1:5) emphasizes that we need to depend on God because we lack godly wisdom and knowledge. Therefore, God gave laws to follow that lead to righteousness (Exod 22; Matt 5–7). God commands us to submit to his will (Jas 4:7) and to follow his will instead of relying on our own planning (Jas 4:15). God has given his Word as a standard to follow for life and health (Exod 34:32; Eccl 12:13; Matt 19:17) and he has given his only Son to provide salvation that cannot be achieved by human effort (John 1:12; 3:16).

3. Saucy, "Theology of Human Nature," 22–23.
4. Hoekema, *Created in God's Image*, 68–73.

God's standard is based on his character of holiness. The Bible repeatedly states that these laws are based on God's holiness and that God is the one who makes us holy (Lev 11:44–45; 1 Pet 1:16). God is the one "who saved us and called us to a holy calling, not because of our works, but because of his own purpose and grace" (2 Tim 1:9).

The substantive view of humanity made in God's image can be seen in our choice to depend on God's wisdom instead of human wisdom (cultural wisdom). When we follow God's wisdom instead of our human wisdom, we reflect God's image and God is glorified.

Functional View—Taking Responsibility for Creation

The functional view of being made in the image of God sees the image of God as taking responsibility for creation (Gen 1:28; Col 1:16–17). Some theologians refer to this aspect as dominion—the responsibility God gave Adam and Eve to rule over and care for the earth and the creatures on the earth (e.g., the fish of the sea, the birds of the air, plants, animals, and human beings) (Gen 1:26–30). God entrusted to us the care of creation as his representatives.[5]

After Adam and Eve disobeyed God's command, they suffered the consequences of their disobedience. Eve was to experience pain in childbearing. Adam was to rule over her (Gen 3:16), but he would have increased labor in working the ground (Gen 3:17). Their disobedience not only affected human relationships with God, it also affected the rest of creation, which is now in bondage to decay (Rom 8:19–20). In order to reverse the effects of sin caused by Adam and Eve's disobedience, God gave his Son the responsibility to reconcile all things back to himself by making peace through his blood shed on the cross (Col 1:20). For this role Christ as the Word became flesh (John 1:14). He is also the way, the truth, and the life (John 14:7). His role not only included the reconciliation of God's relationship with humanity, but also the relationship with creation—the world, plants, animals, and human beings. God's Son set the example for humanity through his life on the earth—his care for creation and his care for humanity. He also gave to believers his ministry of reconciliation (2 Cor 5:18). In order to take care of creation in the way God intended, we need to base our thinking on God's Word and his truth.

5. Ibid., 67.

The functional view of the image of God relates to God the Son's role in taking responsibility and care for creation and can be evaluated on the basis of whether or not what we do and say is in line with God's truth (1 Cor 3:13). When we take responsibility and care for creation in the way God intended, we reflect his image and God is glorified.

Relational View—Loving One Another in Community

Hoekema[6] describes the relational view of the image of God in terms of human relationships with God, others, and creation. Human relationships are described as forming the Body of Christ (1 Cor 12:13) in which the particular roles and functions of believers are like parts of a body that function in unity according to the gifts God has given (1 Cor 12:7). Each person has a gift that enables the whole body to function properly (1 Cor 12:12). Therefore, everyone should have equal concern for one another (1 Cor 12:25) and should honor or treat members that are weaker or considered less honorable with special care (1 Cor 12:22–24). One member cannot say that they do not belong (1 Cor 12:15), and another member cannot say that they do not need other members of the body (1 Cor 12:21).

Human social relationships that reflect the image of God demonstrate a respect for human life (Gen 9:6) and preserve life through words and actions (Jas 3:9). These relationships are also characterized by God-like love (Matt 22:39; Luke 10:27; John 13:35; 15:12; 1 Cor 13; 1 Pet 1:22; 1 John 4:7). This love does not take into account social distinctions such as ethnicity, status, or gender, as all have been made one in Christ (1 Cor 12:13; Gal 3:28); instead, these relationships reflect unity and oneness in Christ (John 17:11; 1 Cor 12; Eph 4:13). The fruit of the Spirit (love, joy, peace, patience, kindness, goodness, faithfulness, gentleness, and self-control) are also evident in these relationships (Gal 5:22–23).

The image of God is reflected through both genders (Gen 1:26–27). One gender by itself is not sufficient to reflect God, but needs the other to fully reflect God. The two gender roles are not to be competitive or to elevate or subjugate the other. Rather, there is to be a mutual submissive relationship to each other based on reverence for Christ (Eph 5:21).

God created us so that his love could flow into us and through us to others (1 John 4:11–12). Love and reverence for God are characterized by certain kinds of responsibilities that foster healthy and godly relationships.

6. Ibid., 75–82.

Husbands are to love and respect their wives and be the head of the wife *as Christ is head of the church* (Eph 5:23–25; 1 Pet 3:7). Wives are to submit to their husbands *as to the Lord* (Eph 5:22; 1 Pet 3:1–6). In the same manner, children should obey their parents *for this is right* (Eph 6:1–3). Fathers are not to exasperate their children, but to bring them up in the training and instruction of the Lord (Eph 6:4). Slaves are to obey their masters with respect, fear, and sincerity of heart, just *as you would Christ* (Eph 6:5–8). Masters are to *do the same to them . . . knowing that he who is both their master and ours is in heaven, and that there is no partiality with him* (Eph 6:9). Obedience is not on the basis of having to be submissive, but on wanting to please God.

We are commanded to be loving, compassionate, humble, living in harmony with each other, and repaying with blessing rather than evil for evil or insult for insult (1 Pet 3:8–9). The believer is to put religion into practice by caring for family members; that is, parents, widows and orphans (Jas 1:27). In this way parents and grandparents are repaid. The family member who does not provide for his or her family is said to have denied the faith (1 Tim 5:8). Older men and women are to be responsible for the younger men and women (Titus 2).

The relational view of humanity created in the image of God enables us to fulfill the roles God has assigned. In this way God's character is reflected in these relationships. God the Holy Spirit guides us into truth (John 16:13). When our behavior is based on the belief that we are made in the image of God, our lives will be characterized by the fruit of the Spirit, by the proper functioning of the Body of Christ, and by God being glorified. God the Holy Spirit guides us and teaches us the things we need to say and do (Luke 12:12; John 14:26; 1 Cor 2:13). When we allow God's Holy Spirit to guide our thoughts and behavior, we reflect the image of God and God is glorified.

How the Image of God Works

Just as God has various characteristics, so we, who are created in his image, also have distinct capacities that God intended to reflect him. The English Scriptures use several words to describe these capacities. We are to love God with our whole being—heart, soul, strength (Deut 6:5); heart, soul, and mind (Matt 22:37); heart, soul, mind, and strength (Mark 12:33, Luke 10:27). The integration of the concepts of "will, mind, and heart" in Hebrew and Greek languages reveal that the "heart" is the center of the self and "the place where faith takes root in both mind and emotion."[7] However, in English the words "will," "mind," and "heart" do not overlap in the same way. As a result, English speakers have difficulty integrating decision-making (will), thinking (mind), and emotions (heart), while speakers of non-English languages such as Chinese, Korean, and Japanese more easily integrate the will, mind, and heart. Speakers of these languages have difficulty understanding the English separation of the parts.

Figure 10 below depicts how humans are created in God's image. As God is composed of the God the Father, God the Son, and God the Holy Spirit, we can reflect God in our will (decision-making), mind (truth), and heart (emotions based on relationships).

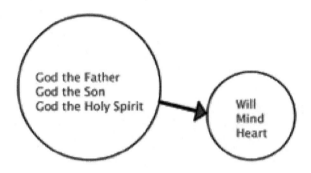

Figure 10: Created in God's Image

The human capacity to make decisions reflects God as the ultimate authority. In English, this capacity has been called the will. As people live together, they create certain kinds of decision-making processes: 1) some groups are characterized by individual decision-making (e.g., the United States); 2) other groups, such as those in Western Europe, establish a system of rules that is diligently followed; while 3) Asians and others follow a hierarchical structure in which the ultimate authority resides at the top and those underneath submit to the will of the leader(s); and 4) in smaller people groups or cultures, decisions are made by group consensus in which every member is given a voice and has the right to speak. In the event of a disagreement,

7. Elliott, *Faithful Feelings*, 131.

individuals in these small societies defer to others in order to maintain a sense of harmony.[8]

When our will is aligned with God's will based on God's Word, we choose God's will over human systems of rules, human decisions made by authority figures, and human group consensus (e.g., Acts 4:19, Peter before the Sanhedrin). If we desire to reflect God's image, we seek God's wisdom in making our everyday decisions. In this way, our will (decision-making) can reflect the image of God.

When we use our human capacity to know truth (the mind) and take responsibility for this truth, we can also reflect God. God's truth encompasses who he is and what he has done for all of creation. However, human knowledge is very limited. Knowledge is also culturally defined. Cultures that focus on the individual consider knowledge and behavior to be separate. In these cultures, each person makes his or her own decisions about what is true. These cultures also base knowledge on scientific facts that can be proven through established procedures. Deviations from scientific facts are not considered to be true knowledge or truth. On the other hand, Asian cultures correlate knowledge with behavior and also view knowledge as that which has passed down from parent to child from generation to generation. Asians define truth as not only what is said, but also what is done. If a person says he or she will do something and does not do it, they are not considered a person of integrity.

However, when we are aligned with God's will, we make decisions based on the truth of God's Word guided by his Spirit and in so doing reflect God's character in our actions and relationships. Then our lives are not limited by cultural perspectives but are characterized by holiness that transcends culture.

The human capacity for relationships (the heart) reflects God's character by creating a true harmonious community. Such a community includes rather than excludes. Human cultures tend to establish certain roles that include some people but exclude others. Some cultures elevate some people over others, as exemplified by Asian cultures that have a defined hierarchy. In Asian cultures, men typically fill the highest leadership roles, while women are expected to submit to their authority. In Asian cultures the first-born son is expected to take care of his mother when his father dies, while in American culture each child has the option to choose who cares or does not care for their mother if their father dies.

8. See chapter 10 for more discussion on harmony.

When our cross-cultural life and ministry interactions align with God's truth, our decision-making helps us function as part of the body of Christ utilizing our God-given spiritual gifts. We accept and develop our spiritual gifts and foster the recognition and appreciation of the gifts of others. We also facilitate unity and the harmonious functioning of the body of Christ. We attend to those who are weaker and encourage them to be strong. We attend to the needs of orphans, widows, and the oppressed (Isa 1:17; Luke 4:18). We encourage the strong to lift up the weak. The fruit of the Spirit is demonstrated in our behavior, and God is glorified (Rom 15:6, 1 Pet 2:12).

Being created in the image of God means that we can reflect God in three ways: 1) substantially, by choosing to align our wills with God in decision-making and not depending on human wisdom; 2) functionally, through taking care of creation based on God's truth, giving God the glory rather than humans; and 3) relationally, through developing loving relationships with one another. The result of the image of God functioning as God intended will be a community where God's character of justice, righteousness, faithfulness, and love make a *shalom* community possible.[9] This *shalom* community practices repentance, forgiveness, and reconciliation;[10] exhibits the fruit of the Spirit; functions as the Body of Christ; and addresses conflicts biblically.

Shalom, the Hebrew word for peace, refers not only to external peace (i.e., the opposite of war), but also to an internal state.[11] The well-being or wholeness of an individual can only be fully realized within the wholeness of the community. Righteousness and justice ensures the general health and well-being of the community as a whole.[12] Platinga explains:

> "The way things ought to be" in its Christian understanding includes the constitution and internal relations of a very large number of entities—the Holy Trinity, the physical world in all its fullness, the human race . . . In a shalomic state each entity would have its own integrity or structured wholeness, and each would also possess many edifying relations to other entities.[13]

---

9. Swartley, "Relation of Justice/Righteousness," 29–30.

10. Turner, "Paul," 77.

11. White, *Shalom*, 4.

12. Waltner, "Shalom," 145.

13. Plantinga, *Not the Way*, 10.

The image of God works to create a *shalom* community in which the physical, emotional, and spiritual well-being of all are addressed. This community would be a place where family relations, as well as cross-cultural and cross-generational teams, can live and work together harmoniously, recognizing the strengths and values in each person and appropriately addressing differences. Platinga notes that a *shalom* community:

> ... would include, for instance, strong marriages and secure children. Nations and races in this brave new world would treasure differences in other nations and races as attractive, important, complementary. In the process of making decisions, men would defer to women and women to men until a crisis arose. Then with good humor all around, the person more naturally competent in the area of the crisis would resolve it to the satisfaction and pleasure of both.[14]

Unfortunately, this is not the way things are. Instead, we experience constant misunderstandings, emotional upheavals, and unresolved conflicts that distort the image of God. That is not the way God intended things to be.

How the Image of God is Distorted

God created us to reflect him, but we also have the capacity to develop our own ways of doing things, as seen in the varieties of human cultures. God created us, so he knows all about us. God knows what kind of relationships would foster and develop his characteristics. God gave the Ten Commandments, the "Golden Rule," and other instructions in Scripture to bring life (Luke 10:27–28). Not following God's commands leads to sickness (Exod 15:26). Being made in God's image means we have the ability to create our own culture, our own way of doing things. These human systems do not always lead to life, health, and prosperity and, therefore, distort the image of God. Whatever does not lead to *shalom* is sin. It "is the disruption or disturbance of what God has designed" and, therefore, does not give glory to God.[15]

We unconsciously distort God's image by following our cultural practices. This occurs when we follow human systems of decision-making rather than God's decision-making, when we uphold human truth rather

14. Ibid., 11.
15. Ibid., 16–17.

than God's truth, and when we do not function as the body of Christ or demonstrate the fruit of the Spirit. We often follow cultural ways that distort, rather than reflect, God's image.

The first chapter of Romans (1:18–32) explains the process involved when the image of God is distorted. First, a decision is made to not glorify to God or to give him thanks (1:21). Then God's truth is exchanged for a lie (1:25). Finally, all kinds of sinful behavior results, including condoning sin (1:29–32). The nature of sin is rebellion against God and his revelation of himself. God allows us to experience the natural consequences of our sin.[16] However, the image of God can be restored, and we can give glory to God by replacing lies with the truth and joining with Christ's ministry of reconciliation (2 Cor 5:18) that involves repentance and forgiveness from God (1 John 1:9) and forgiveness with others (Matt 6:12). This process creates and maintains a *shalom* community.

Knowing and believing we are made in the image of God and that God loves us unconditionally because of what he has done for us, not for what we do for him, is the first step toward untangling the cultural challenges of Asian American life and ministry. When we accept what God has done for us, we are able to accept others as God has accepted us. We are also able to understand how what we say and do can distort God's image in us and in our relationships with others. As a result of believing we are made in God's image, we desire to reconcile ourselves with God and with others by repenting of our wrongful treatment of others and forgiving others when they treat us wrongly.

An Example of a Distorted Image of God[17]

A turning point in my life was when I began to understand what it meant to be created in God's image. That is, that God loves me unconditionally, not based on what I do or do not do, but based on what Jesus did for me on the cross. For many years I felt God was pleased with me when I worked hard. When I went into full-time ministry my father asked me if I was working eight hours a day in ministry. I answered his question believing that working hard was what God wanted me to do. In fact, I believed that the more I worked, the more God was pleased with me.

16. Johnson, "God Gave Them up," 25.
17. These are Sheryl's reflections on being created in the image of God.

My family valued achievement. When I got straights A's in school or received some kind of achievement award, they praised me. I thought God was also especially pleased with me when I did well in school. When I did things to take care of my family and my work, I felt God was also pleased with me, but I also felt I had to do more.

It wasn't until after my first diagnosis with cancer that I began to understand how my false cultural beliefs drove me to do more work than I was physically, emotionally, and spiritually capable of doing. As a result of my drive to work, I experienced a lot of stress, frustration, bitterness, hurt, negative feelings, and anger. I knew these were not godly feelings, but I did not know where they came from because I was doing what I thought God wanted me to do—work.

As I meditated on what it means to be created in the image of God (Gen 1:26-27), I began to realize that I had distorted the image of God with the false cultural belief that God was only pleased with me when I did a lot of things for him. Not only did I believe a lie about myself, I also realized how proud I was of all the things I did. My pride increased when I compared myself to others. I even tried to make others work harder by suggesting ways they could add more work to their already busy schedules. I offended many people with my suggestions that they do more.

My actions did not lead to a *shalom* community. My actions validated my belief that doing a lot of work was the way to please God. I didn't know how to say "no" or to discern if particular opportunities were what God wanted me to do. When I had too many commitments, I couldn't fulfill them well, and doing a poor job made me feel bad about myself. I couldn't see the negative circular reasoning of my false beliefs and I would project my negative feelings on others and make them feel bad as well.

I was distorting God's image in the belief that I had to do a lot of work to please God, therefore my decision-making committed me to do more than I could actually do, and this affected my relationships with God and others. I didn't know that it was my false beliefs based on a cultural type[18] that created a negative downward spiral in my life similar to the pattern described in Romans 1.

In the next chapter we present a theory of culture (Structure and Community) in order to better understand the misunderstandings between the more-Asianized Americans and the more-Americanized Asians.

---

18. See chapter 7 for a more complete discussion of cultural types.

Reflection Questions

1. Describe a situation in your church, ministry, or your life that does not reflect the fruit of the Spirit, the body of Christ, or a *shalom* community.

2. What are some of the beliefs that influence your decision-making and your emotions affecting the relationships in the situation?

3. In what way is God's image (his authority, truth, and relationships) not reflected in your response to others in this situation? Meditate on Gen 1:26-27 and Rev 5:9; 7:9. Spend twenty minutes in prayer and write up some thoughts based on what God is speaking to you about restoring his image in this situation.

7

Understanding Our
Cultural Differences

IN SECTION 1 BEN identified various aspects of Asian life and ministry related to the first generation or more-Asianized Americans and the more-Americanized second-generation Asian Americans. We have seen how the divide between the Asian and American cultures shaped different church models and how American individualism created a desire for more independent church planting. Ben also discussed a misunderstanding of the concept of grace, comparing a Western concept of grace with a more global concept, how honor and shame work, and Chinese and Korean expressions of spirituality. Many of the examples cited came from students who took "The Asian Church in American Society" course offered at Talbot School of Theology over the past twenty-five years.

Ben and I continue to find numerous examples of misunderstandings between the first-generation Asians and the more-Americanized Asians that arise from a lack of understanding of the cultural differences between the two groups. First-generation Asians are perplexed by the fact that Americanized Asians are very informal in their actions and in the way they act and dress, the way they view the world, and how they speak. The Americanized Asians are confused by the hierarchical structure of the first generation, the social expectations of their family and others, and being treated like children even though they are adults. Generally, neither generation is aware of how their own cultural influences contribute to these different expectations. Therefore, they are unable to address or resolve the misunderstandings in a biblical way in order to experience God's grace more fully.

The first challenge in untangling the cultural complexities of the Asian American church in order to experience God's grace involves the discovery of the different underlying cultural beliefs. In the United States there are many definitions of culture, and each person may have a personal definition. Without a common definition of culture it is difficult to talk about culture in such a way that everyone understands what other people are saying. The absence of a common understanding of culture in the United States also makes it difficult to identify and resolve cultural misunderstandings.

Many people have defined culture in terms of values, but values are only part of culture. Culture also includes thinking, actions/behaviors, and feelings.[1] The words for culture in Asian languages refer to everything to do with life: Japanese *bunka* 文化, Chinese *wénhuà* 文化, and Korean *munwha* 문화. In this book, we use the Asian definition of culture—the everyday way of doing things that includes all of life. We will discuss Asian American differences further in chapter 8 when we explore more deeply the underlying sources of differences between Asian and American cultures and how language reinforces these differences.

The main feature that has been used to distinguish Asian and American cultures is the perspective of the person—as an individual or as an integral part of a group. Hofstede's extensive study of fifty countries rated people along five basic dimensions of culture.[2] One of the dimensions was Individualism and Collectivism. He described Individualistic cultures as having a focus on the individual, with loose social ties; while collective cultures have a focus on the family/community/group, with stronger, and more cohesive ties. Individualism stands for a society in which the ties between individuals are loose. Hofstede notes:

> Everyone is expected to look after her/his immediate family only. Collectivism stands for a society in which people from birth onwards are integrated into strong, cohesive in-groups, which throughout people's lifetime continue to protect them in exchange for unquestioning loyalty.[3]

In Hofstede's study Americans were identified as having a high degree of individualism (91),[4] while East Asian countries (China, Japan, Korea)

---

1. Kesler, "Abdication," 306.

2. Hofstede, *Culture's Consequences*, 209–79.

3. Ibid., 225. Individualism and Collectivism were rated along a continuum of 1 to 100. The higher score indicated Individualism while the lower score indicated Collectivism.

4. Hofstede, "Individualism, United States."

scored low on individualism (Japan 46, China 20, South Korea 18).[5] Collective behavior focuses more on the interaction within the group than on individual functioning. Robertson lists six features of collective behavior:

1. Group welfare is more important than individual rewards.

2. Group success is more important than individual success.

3. Being accepted by the members of your work group is very important.

4. Employees should only pursue their goals after considering the welfare of the group.

5. Managers should encourage group loyalty even if individual goals suffer.

6. Individuals may be expected to give up their goals in order to benefit group success.[6]

In the late 1990s the increased economic growth of Asian countries was attributed to "Asian Cultural Values" that were identified as basically Confucian values.[7] These values include strong family ties, respect for authority, the importance of education, hard work, cooperation, and a balance between the individual's needs and those of society.[8] Based on the influence of Confucian values on Asian culture, Hofstede added the Confucian dimension of Long-Term Orientation to his list of cultural values.[9]

The United States has demonstrated a higher rate of Individualism than other countries. Numerous books and articles have pointed out the Individualistic characteristic of American culture.[10] Individualistic tendencies in the U.S. are reinforced by the cultural values inherent in the English language. For example, English speakers make numerous references to the word "self," either by itself or in a phrase. The term "self" is used to form a wide range of expressions including the recent word "selfie," which refers

---

5. Hofstede, "Individualism, Japan"; "Individualism, China"; "Individualism, South Korea."

6. Robertson, *Global Dispersion*, 266.

7. O'Dwyer, "Democracy," 39.

8. Hitchcock, *Asian Values*, 2.

9. Hofstede and Minkor, "Long- versus Short-term," 496.

10. Bellah, *Habits of the Heart*, 142–66; Stewart and Bennett, *American Cultural Ways*, 133–37; Althen, *American Way*, 3–20.

to a person who takes his or her own photo. The modern use of the word "self" in English has replaced the word for "soul."[11]

The cultural dimension of Individualism and Collectivism, however, only describes half of the cultural difference between American and Asian cultures. The other half can be described as Hierarchy as opposed to no common Hierarchy. Hierarchy refers to how people fit into a whole and also how they are categorized by age, status, and gender.

A theory of culture developed by Mary Douglas,[12] a British social anthropologist, has been widely used to help people understand cultural differences, including differences between Asian and American cultures. Douglas's theory of culture has two dimensions—Structure (how people are different) and Community (how people are the same). Differences or distinctions between individuals are referred to as Structure. Differences can be made on the basis of status, age, gender, birth order, ethnicity, color, job position, or other categories. The type of decision-making (individual, system rules, top-down, or consensus) defines Structure. The type of social responsibility (individual responsibility, system responsibility, top down responsibility or group responsibility) defines Community. These two dimensions can be either Strong or Weak or on a continuum from Strong to Weak, forming four basic cultural types—Weak Structure and Weak Community (Individuating; e.g., U.S. Americans[13]), Strong Structure and Weak Community (Institutionalizing; e.g., Europeans, Canadians, and some aspects of American society), Strong Structure and Strong Community (Hierarching; e.g., Asians, Middle Eastern peoples, Latins, Africans, etc.), and Weak Structure and Strong Community (Interrelating; e.g., small egalitarian groups, families, or clans). Douglas's theory of culture is described in greater detail, with illustrations from each of the four cultural types, in *Biblical Multicultural Teams: Applying Biblical Truth to Cultural Differences*.[14]

11. "self," http://dictionary.reference.com/browse/self.

12. Douglas, "Cultural Bias," 183–254. Douglas used the terms "grid" and "group," but the terms "structure" and "community" are used here.

13. The term "American" or "U.S. American" is used to refer to the general cultural features of the U.S. population.

14. Silzer, *Biblical Multicultural Teams*, 21–42. The book was written to enable multicultural team members to discover their cultural self-identity in order to deal with multicultural team misunderstandings. Examples of Individuating, Institutionalizing, Hierarching, and Interrelating cultures are discussed in regard to family structure, nurture and discipline, house floor plans, and household practices such as visiting, eating, working, resting, and cleaning. The book takes people back to their childhood home to revisit how their cultural practices were formed and encourages them to compare

The main concept of the Structure and Community theory of culture is that people live their lives in light of certain beliefs about how things should be done. These beliefs become ingrained over time as they form a pattern of behaviors that become a person's default way of doing things. These patterns shape what is called a person's Culture-based Judging System (CbJS). That is, a person's preferred way of doing things creates a bias towards certain ways of doing things, even among believers. When Christians do things in the same way over a period of time, they tend to interpret their preferred way of doing things as the right and biblical way to do things, even though their actions do not always lead to or result in godly behavior. That is, their responses do not produce the fruit of the Spirit, God's *shalom*, or the proper functioning of the body of Christ in their lives or in the lives of those around them. When believers interact more regularly with people from other cultures, they more easily recognize their own cultural interpretation of doing things and are more willing to make changes in order to further the Kingdom of God on earth.

Douglas says that individuals unconsciously adopt Structure and Community ideals through habit patterns formed by their everyday activities. Although these unconscious cultural ideals are not generally verbalized or discussed, they can be observed in a person's daily behavior patterns and how people respond to different ways of doing things. The Structure and Community theory can help us understand the differences between Asian and American behavior patterns in the Asian American church.

Structure and Community

Structure focuses on differences or distinctions; Community focuses on similarities. Structure sets up differing social roles that focus on the external, material, and physical aspects of people (e.g., family relationships [mother/father, son/daughter], age [older/younger], gender [male/female], etc.). Community, by reinforcing the similarities among individuals, focuses on the internal, immaterial, and spiritual aspects of people. Structure is established and maintained by decision-making type—following the authority system (the rules of the system, the leaders, or group consensus) or making individual decisions. Community is established by participation within a community—upholding the community identity, giving in

their findings with Scripture to see whether their practices result in cultural or biblical behavior.

to community pressure, taking social responsibility for group members, etc. Structure, in differentiating individuals, forms a system of legal justice; Community, in reinforcing similarities of the community, forms a system of social justice. These two perspectives create different bases of morality and can lead to much misunderstanding.

Decision-making in Strong Structure groups follows the rules of the system. In the Strong Structure system there is an established way of doing things or rules that have developed over time. These rules have been formalized into policies and are difficult to change. The system gives power to authority figures to interpret the rules of the system, and people are expected to follow the rules. Therefore, the typical result of a disagreement in Strong Structure cultures is that the system or the leaders win, not the individual. On the other hand, Weak Structure cultures emphasize individual decision-making processes. In Weak Structure cultures individuals find their own sources of information upon which to base their decisions, whereas in Strong Structure cultures the information already exists in the rules of the system, in tradition, or as interpreted by its leaders. When individual decisions are made in Weak Structure cultures, the individual holds the authority, but when Weak Structure individuals disagree, they do not have the support of Strong Structure to resolve a disagreement. When the individual has the authority, the rules are interpreted individually. In Weak Structure cultures individuals have their own opinions and, as a result, there is constant disagreement and conflict. The typical result of conflict in Weak Structure is that the person with more power, resources, or influence wins.

Community refers to the strength of social relationships demonstrated by social cohesiveness and responsibility for community members. Strong Community is based on the belief that individuals are basically spiritual beings connected to a higher power in the universe. Life consists of the group rather than the individual and life functions appropriately when there is harmony among the community members, including their relationship to the created world and even to deceased family members. The spiritual connection in Strong Community groups is demonstrated through ongoing reciprocal relations between individuals, including sharing resources— physical, emotional, spiritual. In Strong Community the image of family relationships (e.g., children to parents) is often used in other areas of life, including the work situation. That is, employees may refer to their superior as their father or mother, and employers may refer to their subordinates as sons or daughters even though they are not family members.

In Strong Community cultures life is viewed as a cycle of significant life events. Life cycle events (birth, puberty, marriage, death), as well as the agricultural calendar (new year, new moon, planting, harvesting, etc.), are celebrated as a community to insure the continuance of harmonious and prosperous life. Community members, by regularly helping one another and reciprocating the help they receive, foster the cycle of life. Not helping or reciprocating can cause bad things to happen. Strong Community individuals, therefore, need to participate regularly in social activities in order to maintain harmony in community life. Good and evil, right and wrong are defined by community participation. Participating and helping others is good and right; not participating or helping others is evil or wrong. Individuals who do not participate in social activities are viewed as inviting or causing misfortune. Individuals who do not participate with the community may also be suspected of manipulating the spirit world through black magic, sorcery, spells, etc. that cause bad things to happen. Therefore, the community takes responsibility for group participation in community activities in order to promote good and to avoid evil.

Families are very important in Strong Community cultures because a person's identity is derived from belonging to a family and/or community. Loyalty is first and foremost to one's family; other affiliations take second place. Individuals in Strong Community spend time together regularly and by so doing demonstrate their loyalty. Resources are shared, and individuals who extend help also expect reciprocal help from others at some time in the future. This reciprocity continues beyond the present generation, thus strengthening family or community ties and relationships.

The four cultural types are illustrated in Figure 11. First, on the bottom left is the Individuating (Weak Structure and Weak Community) cultural type illustrated by ten circles in random arrangement. Above that is the Institutionalizing (Strong Structure and Weak Community) cultural type depicted by a typical organizational chart. The circle at the top identifies the leader (CEO), while the lower levels represent the other people in descending order. In the top right is the Hierarching (Strong Structure and Strong Community) cultural type. The Hierarching culture is similar to the Institutionalizing culture except the circles are touching and enclosed in a larger circle indicating Strong Community. On the bottom right is the Interrelating (Weak Structure and Strong Community) cultural type, also enclosed by a Strong Community circle, but without the hierarchic distinctions (Weak Structure), representing everyone as the same or equal.

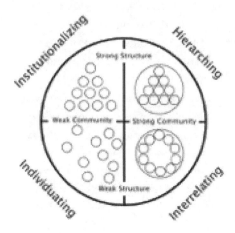

Figure 11: Four Cultural Types

Each of the four cultural types has a different kind of decision-making, based on a different type of truth, and either a weak or a strong sense of social responsibility (as a result of Community). Because people are made in God's image, they can either follow biblical ways to reflect God's image or they can distort God's image by following cultural ideals. When a person strongly holds to their cultural way of doing things, they respond negatively to other ways of doing things. Their Culture-based Judging System (CbJS) responses justify and uphold their cultural beliefs. The CbJS operates when a person makes repeated judgments (with words or actions) of what is right and what is wrong in order to validate their own way of doing things. Such a pattern is a natural human response to dealing with differences. Even though a person's words may not sound like a judgment, what is said highlights the difference—a different way of speaking, interacting, eating, working, etc. The resulting actions also indicate a judgment of right or wrong through avoidance, delay of interaction, criticism, or even retaliation. The reason someone points out the difference is to validate his or her own cultural way of doing things.

Douglas also says that each cultural type is part of a whole—the strengths of one type are the weaknesses of the other types. The theory as a whole provides an illustration of how the image of God works. Each cultural type creates a typical sin that is shaped by the cultural ideal, but the people within that cultural type generally do not recognize their sin. When a person encounters a different cultural way of doing things, he has an opportunity to discover his cultural preferences and to compare his responses to how the body of Christ is meant to function. We will examine each of the four cultural types in detail in the next sections.

Individuating Culture

Individuating cultural practices reflect fewer common social differentiations (Weak Structure) and less social similarity (Weak Community). The ideal for the Individuating person is the individual who prefers making individual decisions based on a personal understanding of truth and also prefers choosing the kind of social responsibility they take for others. Americans are typically identified as Individuating because they prefer individual choice. The ability to make individual decisions is considered an individual and inalienable right, and choice is considered to be something that each person should have. The Individuating person also makes individual decisions in regard to their personal identity and in the way they want to characterize their own personality or reputation. Their individual decisions reinforce their identity; how people spend their time and their money reveals their individuality.

As a child, an Individuating person is trained to make his or her own decisions. Their parents may ask them what they like and what they don't like, what they want to do and what they don't want to do. At an early age, Individuating children learn to make their own decisions about what they like or don't like. Individuating people also prefer to choose their level of social responsibility.[15] Some people are willing to take social responsibility and to care for family members or others; others are not. For an Individuating person, the choice to help others or not to help others is what makes the Individuating person unique. They do not believe that another person has the right to expect their help unless it is freely offered. Innovation and creativity are also highly valued in this type. A person in an Individuating culture believes he or she loses their individuality if they are the same as others.

An Individuating person can reflect the image of God by making an individual decision to align his or her will with God's will based on God's Word. They can also choose to follow God's direction in the kind of social responsibility they take for others. When they follow God's will, their own

15. Naylor, *American Culture*, 51.

will, mind, and heart can reflect the image of God. On the other hand, their Individuating cultural ideal values individual decisions that may not be aligned with God's will but are based on individualized truth they have found or heard from others. They also prefer to make their own decisions regarding the kind of social responsibility they take for others. In this way Individuating people can individually reflect or distort the image of God.

The typical sin of the Individuating person is greed, which is reflected in self-pride, with little or no responsibility for others.[16] Individuating people reinforce their ideal by talking about themselves in order to enhance their individual identity. They believe that acquiring the latest technology, clothing, car, etc. enhances their individual identity. Individuals also take advantage of opportunities to get ahead. The Individuating person's desire for control can easily lead a person to take advantage of others, to hurt others, or to cause others to lose out. These behaviors help the individual to get ahead and are not considered wrong because the self-focus of the Individuating person or people does not take into consideration how their actions affect others.[17]

Individuating people get upset, frustrated, or angry (that is, their Individuating CbJS kicks in) when something bad happens that does not uphold their individual identity.[18] For example, if an Individuating person's ideal is to get good grades, they might get upset when they receive a bad grade. Their response to the bad grade might be to blame whomever or whatever they believe stopped them from achieving their ideal. They may blame themselves, other people, their teachers, the assignment, etc. They might challenge the teacher about the grade or try to explain their situation (e.g., they were sick, their computer crashed, their roommate made too much noise, etc.). Additionally, Individuating people do not like to be classified with others as a group, because a collective identity goes against the individuating ideal. Most Americans will deny that they have a common culture or that they share the same cultural ideals as other Americans.[19]

It is difficult, however, to maintain an Individuating culture if everyone does what they want to do without regard for others. This would lead to chaos. Therefore, institutions have been developed to help Individuating people regulate their choices and to provide some societal order. Even in

---

16. Douglas, *Risk and Blame*, 145.

17. Wilkins and Sanford, *Hidden Worldviews*, 42.

18. Stewart and Bennett, *American Cultural Patterns*, 63.

19. Naylor, *American Culture*, 22.

the U.S., an individual has to conform to institutions such as the local government, a school, a church, or a corporation, yet they can still choose to move to another area or try to figure out how to get around the rules that they do not like. People can also choose to affiliate with other institutions (e.g., church, social club, sports group, etc.).[20]

Institutionalizing Culture

Institutionalizing cultural practices are characterized by a common system of social differentiations/distinctions (Strong Structure) with little social similarity (Weak Community). Social distinctions can come from social class or from individual achievement (e.g., people who demonstrate some kind of skill or ability are placed above those who do not have those skills or abilities). The ideal person in this type of culture is an individual whose identity comes from following the rules of the system and from obeying authority figures, rather than an identity defined by relationships with others or by making his or her own decisions. By following the rules an Institutionalizing person maintains an identity that keeps interaction with others to a minimum. The purpose of the structure is to create an environment in which life and work can be accomplished by following policies that clarify or reduce uncertainty and guide people's expectations.[21] Institutionalizing people prefer getting things done properly, whether in work situations or in other activities such as cooking, eating, and cleaning. Institutions have a "cubicle" mentality in which everyone does his or her own thing in their enclosed space and are generally unaware of what others do. Most Institutionalizing offices assign individuals in lower positions to windowless cubicle work cells, while those in higher positions have larger offices, often with windows. The cubicle walls minimize social distractions and maximize work potential. Institutionalizing people tend to be very organized and like things to be explained clearly. If the rules of the system do not clarify how people are to choose between options, individuals often have difficulty making a decision.

Institutionalizing people can reflect the image of God by following God's law and taking God's direction for social responsibility. However, when they assume that the rules and policies of their organization are what

---

20. Douglas, *Risk and Blame*, 58.
21. Douglas, *How Institutions Think*, 48.

God wants and do not consider the negative consequences that the rules might have on other people, they can individually distort the image of God.

The typical sin in Institutionalizing cultures is to silently accept the consequences of the system rather than speak out against injustices that the system creates.[22] Institutionalizing cultures focus on upholding a system. People in these cultures do not question the rules of the system because they believe the system takes care of all of life. When things go wrong for the Institutionalizing person, they cannot blame the system because the Institutionalizing person's identity is based on the existence of the system. If an individual disagrees with the rules, he or she is challenging his or her own identity. Therefore, people typically do not speak up about injustices because their assumption is that the rules of the system cover every aspect of life.

Institutionalizing people get upset, frustrated, or angry (i.e., their Institutionalizing CbJS kicks in) when something bad happens that does not uphold their Institutionalizing identity. For example, they may get upset if they feel they have fulfilled all the requirements for an assignment and turned it in on time, but the teacher gives them a bad grade. The Institutionalizing person might follow the appropriate procedure to appeal for a grade change, but most likely whoever has followed the appropriate procedures will win unless the leader interprets the rules differently. The way the system works creates fatalism among Institutionalizing people because procedures can change without notice, and there is usually nothing that can be done about not following appropriate procedures. There is also a long list of procedures for making changes. The English axiom "You can't fight City Hall" is illustrative of this fatalistic perspective.

Hierarching Culture

Hierarching cultures are characterized by more social differences (Strong Structure) and more similarities (Strong Community). This type of culture has a centralized structure of individual units that form levels that in turn form an organized whole. Each unit has a head (leader), and the members in each unit ideally support the decision of the head, and the head reports to the next level up. Although Hierarching is similar to Institutionalizing, Hierarching individuals find their identity through belonging to the community that upholds traditions, rather than through following a system of

22. Douglas, *Risk and Blame*, 145.

rules that are there to protect them. Their identity is reinforced by regular participation in activities that reinforce community identity (unlike the lonely person in Individuating and Institutionalizing cultures). People in a Hierarching culture know their place in the hierarchy and behave according to the expectation of their status and role. The Hierarching person (Strong Structure and Strong Community) prefers following the direction of the group's leader based on the traditions of the community. The Strong Community system also takes social responsibility for each member of the community. People in such a group prefer to do things together in an orderly manner that follows the traditional ways of doing things. The people in the community take responsibility for others in the community to ensure that everyone follows the traditions of the community. That is, the group will freely tell someone when he or she is not living up to group expectations. For example, when a single person is old enough to be married, they will continually be asked when they are going to get married. The group fosters conformity by putting pressure on group members, either verbally or by indirect actions. Any older person can tell a younger person what to do and can point out if they are not doing something the right way. The younger people are not allowed to disagree directly with older people, especially their parents. Inequality is part of the definition of the hierarchy, but Strong Community fosters harmony and respect for persons. This combination of Strong Structure and Strong Community is found more frequently in kin-based economic cultures (e.g., cooperatives of ethnic communities such as traditional Japanese, Korean, some Chinese communities, as well as the Old Testament Israelites).[23]

The Hierarching person, particularly the leader, has the potential to reflect the image of God not only as an individual but also corporately because he or she can influence everyone in the group to seek God's direction based on God's Word. Hierarching leaders value taking responsibility for everyone in their group and can encourage group members to follow God and to grow in their relationship with him. On the other hand, Hierarching leaders can be influenced by the authority and power invested in their position and make decisions for their own benefit, thus distorting the image of God. Group members can force others to conform to human standards of behavior rather than God's standard or to hide their resentment of authority figures and rebel against their authority, and thus distort the image of God in the process.

23. Wildavsky, *Nursing Father,* 123–51.

The typical sin in a Hierarching culture is unhealthy community pride; that is, an ingroup versus outgroup pride.[24] Douglas says that this type, the Hierarching culture, in focusing on the good of the community, can often lead to a kind of inappropriate community pride, which tempts its leaders to enhance their own position through getting a greater share of the resources.

When something goes wrong that doesn't uphold the Hierarching ideal, Hierarching people may get upset, frustrated, or angry (i.e., their Hierarching CbJS kicks in). For example, parents whose ideal is for their children to get good grades in order to uphold the parents' reputation in the group can get upset, frustrated, or angry when their child gets a bad grade. The parents would try to make the child feel shame because the bad grade caused the family or community to lose face or to be dishonored. The parents might also put pressure on the teacher to change the grade by inviting him or her to dinner or by giving them a gift. Although the parental request would not be verbalized, a Hierarching teacher would understand that the parents' actions require reciprocity and, in this case, be influenced to give the student a better grade.

Interrelating Culture

Interrelating cultural practices are characterized by a combination of less social differentiation (Weak Structure) and more similarities (Strong Community). This cultural type differs from Hierarching in that there is little or no stratified structure. Instead, each individual is considered equal to the others. Everyone is considered a brother or sister, even though older people might be referred to as mother or father. This type typically has traditional complementary concepts such as male/female, sacred/secular, etc. The Interrelating type seeks to maintain equality through dialogue and sharing. Such a community reacts against organizational rules, regulations, and authority figures. The Interrelating person (Weak Structure and Strong Community) prefers to follow the consensus of the group based on group participation in making decisions. If group members are not allowed to give their opinion, they don't feel valued within the group. Interrelating cultures also put pressure on group members to conform to group decisions. They generally treat everyone as equal. The early Christian church

24. Douglas, *Risk and Blame*, 145.

life described in the book of Acts has been described as a combination of Weak Structure and Strong Community.[25]

The Interrelating group has the potential to reflect the image of God if the group members all come to consensus to seek God's will based on his Word. Their Strong Community interactions put pressure on group members to conform. In this way the whole group can reflect God's image, as opposed to Weak Community where the individual influences only him- or herself. People in an Interrelating group can all distort the image of God if they make a community decision that is not aligned with God's will or based on his Word or they can all have the potential to reflect his image.

Douglas says that the typical sin of Interrelating culture is envy. People in Interrelating cultures easily recognize inequalities and constantly try to equalize situations and resources so that their ideal of equality can be maintained.[26] The Interrelating ideal is violated when resources are not equally shared or reciprocated. Because equality is the ideal in this type, any form of inequality, particularly as demonstrated by the Individuating, Institutionalizing, or Hierarching cultural type, is seen as opposing the group ideal and needing correction. Harmony arises from equality, and equality is demonstrated through the sharing of resources.

When something goes wrong for Interrelating people that blocks their ideals, they can get upset, frustrated, or angry (i.e., their Interrelating CbJS kicks in). An example of something bad happening is when one person is singled out for some reason, such as getting a better grade than others or is honored for an achievement. When this happens the other group members might criticize the person who stands out in order to bring the person back down to the same level. Another example is when a child is not allowed to graduate with his peers. In such a case the whole group would enter into the process of righting this wrong or lack of equality.

How the Four Cultural Types Interact

A major issue for Asian Americans is the difference between Strong and Weak Community. Asians from a Strong Community culture have a group identity rather than an individual identity. Their cultural goal is to ensure that the good reputation or "face"[27] of the group continues. Because the

25. Atkins, *Egalitarian Community*, 148–68.

26. Douglas, *Risk and Blame*, 145.

27. See chapter 10 for a more complete discussion of "face."

same concept of face is not found in American culture, many Americans (and some Asian Americans) are virtually unaware of the positive aspects of this cultural practice, and some non-Asians even condemn the practice as deceitful or sinful.[28]

Individualistic Americans derive their identity from who and what a person is or can do as an individual; Asians derive their identity from who and what people are as a member of the group.[29] In Individualistic cultures each person can make their own decisions, whereas in collective cultures the group arrives at a decision that everyone supports. In fact, it is difficult to go against what the group has decided because collective people tend to conform to the expectations of the group. Triandis notes:

> In individualist societies people are autonomous and independent from their in-groups; they give priority to their personal goals of their in-groups, they behave primarily on the basis of their attitudes rather than the norms of their in-groups, and exchange theory adequately predicts their social behavior.[30]

In collectivistic cultures, it is very important how individuals relate to one another in order to maintain the reputation of the group. It is necessary to know one's social role and behave according to that role. Flanders says "face is a relational, public dimension of self that seeks community acceptance and esteem."[31] Ho explains face as:

> . . . the respectability and/or deference that a person can claim for him/herself from others, by virtue of the relative position he occupies in the social network and the degree to which he is judged to have functioned adequately in the position as well as acceptably in his social conduct.[32]

Cardon and Scott state that "face relates to a person's image and status within a social structure."[33] Ho explains:

> The relational self has an extraordinarily high sensitivity towards the existence of others. The experience of self and others in one's

28. Flanders, "Fixing the Problem," 13.

29. Triandis, "Individualism-Collectivism," 909.

30. Ibid., 909.

31. Flanders, *About Face*, 55–56.

32. Ho, "On the Concept of Face," 883.

33. Cardon and Scott, "Chinese Business Face," 10.

phenomenological world is merged to the extent that they may be separated from the world to form a self-in-relation-with-others.[34]

In Individuating cultures the reputation of the individual is more important than the reputation of the group. Therefore, the concept of face in a collective culture is easily misunderstood in Individuating cultures.

For the Individuating person the closest concept to face is the "self," but this is not defined by a person's social role.[35] Sociologist Goffman says the self is "the positive social value a person claims for himself by the line others assume he has taken during a particular contact."[36] As such, the self can change over time due to life cycle changes or by coping mechanisms that shape one's personality.[37]

Markus and Kitayama[38] describe the difference between Individuating and collective cultures as having an "independent view" versus an "interdependent view" of the self respectively. That is, the independent view of the self is based only on the individual's perception of who he or she is as an individual. Individualistic cultures also "emphasize the task of the presentation while the collective cultures emphasize the task of response to data from social space."[39]

On the other hand, the interdependent (collective) view of the self is based on the social perception of who a person is based on their social role, particularly in regard to family relationships. Markus and Kitayama[40] also explain how these two views greatly affect cognition, emotion, and motivation. The independent view (Individuating) of the self is not dependent on a social context, but the interdependent view of the self is. That is, knowledge or cognition of people from an interdependent view depends on various aspects of the situation (e.g., who is older, male, higher status, etc.), while an independent view of the self does not. As a result, a person's knowledge affects emotions and motivations in different ways. It is easy for people from an independent view of self to misunderstand those from an interdependent view of the self and vice versa.

34. Ho, "Relational Orientation," 160.

35. Marsella et al., "Introduction," 6.

36. Goffman, "On Facework," 213.

37. Markus and Kitayama, "Culture and the Self," 226.

38. Ibid., 246.

39. Persons, *Face Dynamics*, 29.

40. Markus and Kitayama, "Culture and the Self," 224–53.

In the American Individualistic culture no two people are considered to be alike. Each person prefers to be known for his or her individual accomplishments, personality characteristics, and skills, as well as for making their own decisions. Standing out is what gets a person ahead in life. In American culture "the squeaky wheel gets the grease."[41] In collective cultures everyone is similar because they belong to the same group. People like to be known as belonging to the group and do not like to stand out. The Japanese have a saying: "The nail that stands out gets pounded down."[42] Additional details about how Asian face works will be explained in chapter 10.

The first step in addressing the lack of grace in Asian American lives and ministries is to understand how Hierarching Asian cultural differences and Individuating American cultural values create the complexities that need to be untangled in order for God's grace to be experienced. When Individuating Americanized Asians and Hierarching Asians both realize how their responses to the daily challenges they face are a result of their cultural type, they are more willing to reconsider what God wants them to do differently in order to allow God's grace to be experienced in their lives and ministry. Chapter 8 further clarifies the cultural complexities based on different definitions of the person—"I" or "we." A brief look at the various grammatical structures reveals how English and East Asian languages (Chinese, Japanese, and Korean) reflect and uphold their cultural ideals.

Reflection Questions

1. Think of a recent situation that frustrated you in your life and/or ministry and explain if your response came from one of the four cultural ideals: Individuating, Institutionalizing, Hierarching, or Interrelating.

2. In what ways are/were your decision-making, thinking, and relating in conflict with the other people in the situation?

3. Explain how your Culture-based Judging System was evident in the frustrating situation.

4. Meditate on Rom 10:12 and Gal 3:26–29. Spend twenty minutes in prayer and write down some notes based on what God is speaking to you about as a result of your reflective prayer.

41. Ibid., 224.
42. Ibid., 224.

8

Languages Reflect and
Support Cultural Values

CHAPTER 8 ADDRESSES THE cultural complexities that arise from the intersection of American culture (Weak Structure and Weak Community) and Asian culture (Strong Structure and Strong Community). In particular, it explains how the basic difference of the definition of the person as "I" or "we" contributes to the cultural complexities. Understanding this major difference and how it shapes the two cultural ways of thinking will help us untangle the complexities in order that the grace of God can be more fully experienced in the Asian American church.

Americanized Asians are influenced by Individuating cultural values, and Asianized Americans are influenced by Hierarching cultural values. These two cultural values can be described as completely opposite. When both sides believe their own way is biblical, there is no resolution until both realize how their preference for doing things is actually cultural and not biblical.

Different Definitions of the Person

American culture is based on the cultural ideal of the individual; Asian culture is based on the cultural ideal of the family, group, or community. Therefore, the perspective on everything in life comes from a completely different viewpoint, and each culture seeks to address misunderstandings from a cultural perspective, compounding these misunderstandings.

English reflects the influence of the Greek philosophers such as Plato, who defined the person as made up of two parts: the body and the soul or spirit. The French philosopher Descartes referred to the body as a machine that is distinct from the mind or soul. These Western definitions of the person separate the physical world from the spiritual world. The physical world can be categorized, divided, and described in terms of its characteristics; the spiritual world is considered to be separate from the physical world and includes feelings, emotions, and mental activities. The American perspective of the physical or material world has led to a focus on science and the scientific way of establishing truth—that is, trial and error or positing a hypothesis and then determining whether or not the hypothesis is true. American thinking focuses on an analysis of data and formulates models, methods, and principles that can be abstracted and applied to various situations. That is, information about the material world enables the scientist to make generalizations by means of logic.[1]

Americans and other Weak Community cultures define a person as an autonomous individual who has achieved their identity through the things they have individually said and done. Although native English speakers receive help from others, it is not necessary to recognize that help but only to demonstrate an individual's own abilities, skills, and accomplishments. Not acknowledging others' help is the complete opposite of the Asian perspective of a person, who is an integral part of the collective (whole) in which everything one says and does affects the others in the group. In America dualism leads to the expectation for "strong confrontation of opposing views."[2]

The philosophical basis for Asian cultures comes from Confucian, Buddhist, and Taoist thinking in which the world is viewed as an integrated whole of the physical and spiritual.[3] This integrative view not only shapes Asian cultures, it is also maintained by Asian languages. Ho states:

> In the West, there is growing awareness of the tension between two conceptions: The first, rooted in individualism, is that of the autonomous self; the second, more relationally and socially concerned, is that of the self as viewed in terms of engagement with others.[4]

In Strong Community cultures, children are born indebted to their parents for their existence, just as their parents were indebted to their parents, etc. Just as parents nurture and provide care for their children, children, when

1. Stewart and Bennett, *American Cultural Patterns*, 41.
2. Rösch and Segler, "Communication with Japanese," 257.
3. Poškaitė, "Treatment of Human Body," 259.
4. Ho, "On the Concept of Face," 867.

they get older, can reciprocate this care in order for life to continue in a harmonious way. When Americanized Asians identify themselves as an individual whose identity is a result of what they have done rather than what their parents or others have done for them, they bring shame to their parents. This shame is not just personal shame but also a public shame in not upholding the basic Asian value of the family and the family's reputation.

The contrasting definitions of the person affect the interactions of the two groups in every area of life and ministry. One major area is decision-making. The Individuating American believes he or she has the right to make their own decisions and to take individually chosen responsibility for his or her actions. They do not believe that their decisions affect others nor do they believe that others have the right to challenge their decisions. On the other hand, Asian decision-making is top-down. That is, the oldest male in the situation has the right to make decisions. Typically, his decisions are supported by the group and are not questioned because to do so would bring him and the group shame. This clash in decision-making not only happens with one's parents, but also with church leaders or anyone who is older. If younger Asians disagree with older Asians' decisions, they are expected to submit to the decisions, at least outwardly.

Therefore, Americanized Asians become perplexed and/or frustrated when their parents, pastors, or elders request something at the last minute and they are not allowed to refuse or to give a reason why they cannot fulfill the request. On the other hand, parents, pastors, and older people get upset or frustrated when their requests are not quietly accepted and fulfilled. The older Asians view the Americanized Asians as being disrespectful, disloyal, and ungrateful.

In American culture, children are trained from an early age to make decisions regarding what they like and what they do not like. These decisions range from what to eat and what to do, as well as what to wear.[5] When children move out of their parents' house, graduate from high school, get a driver's license, or go off to college, they are considered adults who can make their own decisions. Therefore, American college students and young adults, both single and married, are easily angered if they are not given the opportunity to make their own individual decisions or to express what they think. In American culture, if an individual does not have an opinion on a given issue, they are considered weak.

5. Stewart and Bennett, *American Cultural Patterns*, 63.

However, in an Asian context, age and gender determine who can make decisions. A person (no matter his or her age or marital status) obediently does what an older person requests, and it is not necessary to consider their personal desires.

This Asian definition of the person shapes different expectations for how family members relate to each other. Americanized Asians are perplexed when their parents ask them to visit them but do not talk to them when they are home.[6] They anticipate that their parents will ask them about what they are doing or ask their opinion on some topic. However, people in Hierarching cultures, such as Asians, do not typically talk about themselves, but rather about group activities and they may be content to sit and not talk, but to just be together. It is acceptable for parents to boast about their children, but not to talk about themselves. Americanized Asians are not used to sitting quietly and are quite perplexed when they are not asked about themselves or for their opinion.[7] Clearly the clash of cultures is at work.

When Asian and American cultures clash, the misinterpretation of cultural values and ideals affect relationships. That is, what was expected to be a strong relationship in the Asian culture is often reinterpreted as an individual preference in the American culture. When Asian American children or young people make individual choices, Asian parents and elders are shocked and upset. They do not understand why their requests are not always fulfilled and they feel shamed. Therefore, they feel justified in getting angry at their children. The Americanized Asians do not understand why they cannot make an individual decision, disagree with an older person, or have their explanations accepted. They, in turn, feel justified in getting angry at their parents.

From the perspective of Asians, this clash results in broken relationships and the accompanying emotional state that is embodied in the Korean concept of *han*[8] that occurs when "personal relatedness is neglected and disconnected."[9] *Han* is subjective and difficult to access from an Individuating perspective because it is a collective emotion that grows over time. That

6. Kim, "Expression of Emotions," 41.

7. Mizutani and Mizutani, "How to Be Polite," 117–18.

8. *Han* comes from a Chinese word *hen* which means "to hate or feel resentment: in Japanese *kon* (*urami*) is to bear a grudge." The word also means a desire for revenge. Kim, "Healing of Han," 126.

9. Kwon, "Co-dependence and Interdependence," 46.

is, Americanized Asians might have a history of disagreement with their parents that justifies a strong reaction from them towards their children. As *han* is a phenomenon of a collective community, it "needs a communal conversation to be recognized."[10]

How Language Interacts with Culture

This major difference between the Asian and the American definition of the person is also maintained by language and communication styles. From the perspective of an individual, the English language enables a person to establish their identity by expressing their opinion on a variety of topics. What they say does not necessarily have to be accurate or true; it is regarded as an opinion. English speakers are not typically concerned about offending others, but only about expressing their opinions. They feel that if the other person is offended that is the other person's problem and not the speaker's problem. On the other hand, from the perspective of the family or group, speakers of Asian languages do not establish their identity by expressing their own opinions but by saying things that express respect for the hierarchy and the group way of doing things. The major focus of what they say is shaped by how others might respond or react to what they say as well as how they say it.

Being concerned how others might react reflects the integrated (Asian) view of the person, while not being concerned about how others might react reflects the separate (American) view of the person. In fact, English has been viewed by some people as destroying the Asian way of thinking and communicating because of the way it defines the person. Not only is much lost in translation, there are also many basic concepts in Asian culture that cannot be adequately translated into English.[11] Examples will be given below.

The Individuating cultural type, along with the English language, is said to foster a direct communication style in which the focus is on the individual expressing their thoughts and opinions from their own perspective. On the other hand, the Strong Community Hierarching cultural type, as reflected in Asian languages, is said to foster an indirect communication style in which the focus is on people saying things that harmonize relationships as well as show respect to the hierarchy. Because English speakers view

10. Oh, "Transforming Han," 1102.

11. De Mente, *Chinese Mind*, 30.

the world as separate from themselves, they categorize, analyze, and take apart the things in their world. Based on this kind of analysis they come up with principles and models that help predict how other things in the world operate. This methodology is also used to develop scientific studies.[12] For Asian language speakers, the world cannot be isolated into its various parts but is seen as integrated. Asians also believe that what happens in nature affects people and people affect nature, even though the interaction cannot be explained clearly. Things happen as the result of yin-yang forces that are constantly changing and interacting with each other.[13] (See chapter 10 for more discussion on this topic.)

These two contrasting views of the person are deeply embedded in language—in the speech styles, words, word order, writing systems, use of questions, etc. Although linguists do not consider Chinese, Japanese, and Korean to be related linguistically,[14] they share a number of language and culture similarities that justify grouping them together in this discussion. They also share many of the same characteristics that differ with English.

Speech Styles

English sentences focus on who is doing what. That is, they identify the Subject of the sentence followed by verbs that describe the Subject's action.[15] Sentences in Chinese, Japanese, and Korean focus on comments that are made about a certain Topic or theme. In a Subject-focused language, the Subject is the most basic element, while in Topic-focused languages such as Chinese, Japanese, and Korean, the Topic is the most basic element.[16]

This means that in these Asian cultures communication revolves around situations and social contexts in which relationships are in focus, while in English the communication revolves around the identity that the individual wishes to create for themselves. What they know and do reflects who they are. In Asian languages the family and relationships are in focus. This includes the people in the present as well as the ones who are not present and even the ones who are deceased.

---

12. Nesbitt, *Geography of Thought*, 4, 10.
13. Ibid., 13.
14. Sohn, "State of the Art," 30.
15. Shi, "Topic and Topic Comment," 382–408.
16. Li, *Subject and Topic*, 460.

When an Asian (Chinese, Japanese, Korean) speaks, they are expected to acknowledge their place in the hierarchy through the use of the proper speech style and by using honorific forms (terms of respect). Lu et al. explain:

> A speaker of an Asian language (e.g., Chinese, Japanese, and Korean) is required to evaluate and acknowledge his or her sense of place in a given context based on social rules regarding hierarchy, power, age, and occasion (e.g., formal vs informal).[17]

According to Brown, Korean has six different speech styles (polite, deferential, familiar, semi-formal, plain, and intimate) and Japanese has two (inside vs outside).[18] Mencius[19] encouraged the Chinese not to use first and second person pronouns in addressing others unless they were familiar or intimate. Instead he said they should use surnames, titles, or respectful phrases. Mencius also said that Chinese could also use kin terms such as "aunt" or "uncle" with those who were not blood-related.[20] The context of the social situation determines which of these styles and words or phrases are to be used, as well as the relationships involved that indicate status.[21] For example, when a speaker of an Asian language is talking to a person directly, they use one style and when they are talking about someone else they use another style. If the person is higher status, the person of lower status uses the more polite form if the context is more formal. However, if a person of lower status is psychologically close to the higher-status person or more familiar with him, they may use the familiar form.[22] A person may also switch from one style to another in the middle of speaking in order to indicate a change in their closeness to the topic or to the ones addressed.[23]

In English-speaking cultures, with the focus on the individual, there is normally no need to reference one's place in the social hierarchy, to speak in a formal way, or to use different speech styles unless speaking to someone in a very high political office. The norm for English speakers is to speak about one's own achievements or preferences rather than speaking about

---

17. Lu et al., "Looking up to Others," 77.
18. Brown, "Contrasts Between Korean and Japanese Honorifics," 375.
19. Mencius was an ancient Chinese Confucian philosopher.
20. Hong, "Politeness," 205.
21. Matsumoto and Okamoto, "Construction of the Japanese Language," 35.
22. Choo, "Teaching Language Styles," 87.
23. Brown, "Contrasts Between Korean and Japanese Honorifics," 374.

others unless it is for comparison with one's self. Otherwise talking about others can be considered gossip or a violation of that person's privacy. Because each English speaker develops his or her own way of doing things, there is also no standard behavior based on a social role; rather, each person decides what they want to say and how they want to act in a particular situation. They normally do not have to be fearful of offending others with their speech or their actions because they believe each person is responsible only for themselves.

In Strong Community cultures, such as Asian cultures, there is a much longer history of social interaction and so the body of shared information continues to increase over time. In such cultures a situation does not have to be described completely. Rather people make more use of shortened or coded words or phrases to refer to information they share and use frequently. Strong Community people talk about each other in order to uphold the ideals of the group. It is a kind of social pressure. On the other hand, English speakers do not necessarily need to remember past conversations or incidents in order to express what they think or to give their opinion. Conversations in English do not depend on a history of shared information nor do English speakers need to monitor others' behavior in order to uphold their Individuating cultural ideal.

Words

According to Nisbett, not only do cultures have different preferences for types of speaking styles, cultures also have different preferences for words. Nesbitt reports that English-speaking infants learn nouns more rapidly than other types of words due to the cultural importance of categorizing objects, while Asian infants learn more verbs due to the cultural importance of relationships and describing situations.[24] Zhang and Baker conclude that English speakers listen to the content of what is being said, but Asian speakers listen to how something is said.[25]

Asian words normally contain much more cultural information than English words. For example, words in Asian languages can indicate the level of politeness, formality, social status, as well as emotional content of specific relational situations.

24. Nisbett, *Geography of Thought*, xix.
25. Zhang and Baker, *Inside the Chinese Mind*, 470.

With the focus on the integration of both the body and spirit in Asian cultures, words that have both a physical and spiritual meaning are difficult to translate or understand in English. For example, the word *seishin* in Japanese has been described in terms of mind, spirit, and spiritual education. Spiritual education also includes such activities as judo or flower arranging.[26] Others have translated *seishin* in terms of being the opposite of modern thinking. Austin notes:

> *Seishin* is opposite to modernization . . . it is not democratic, not universalistic, not individualistic, not materialistic. It is rather the complex of loyalty, esprit de corps and indomitable perseverance that is central to so many of the historical accomplishments of Japanese civilization, from art to economic growth.[27]

The integration of body and spirit in Asian languages creates more emotional words to describe relationships than are found in English. Japanese has eleven different words that indicate the emotions arising from the various expectations of relationships. These emotions include the emotion of reliance on the other,[28] often depending on who is in the higher or the lower position.[29] In Korean the word *mianhada* (sorry) contains the meaning of both regret and apology. It is used for "thank you" to show gratitude for a kind deed but also regret for the trouble that it caused the other person.[30] In Japanese the word *sumimasen* can be translated as "thank you," "I'm grateful," "I'm sorry," or "I apologize" due to the additional implication of indebting the receiver.[31] Maynard suggests that when these words are translated into English, they lose their underlying emotional meaning that is present in Japanese.[32]

Markus and Kitayama[33] describe the difference between Asian and American cultures in terms of the focus of the emotions. They argue that in Asia, people view their emotions in terms of what is called "other-focused emotions." The authors suggest that emotions in the two cultures may be similar in some ways, but the focus is entirely different. Emotions in

26. Wierzbieka, "Japanese Key Words," 377.

27. Austin, *Japan*, 255.

28. Markus and Kitayama, "Culture and the Self," 237.

29. Ibid., 239.

30. Kim, "Expression of Emotions," 46.

31. Benedict, *Sword and the Chrysanthemum*, 106.

32. Maynard, "Grammar with an Attitude," 217.

33. Markus and Kitayama, "Culture and the Self," 235.

Asia have another person in mind, but emotions in America (expressed in English) focus on the individual who experiences the emotion. Markus and Kitayama list a number of other-focused emotions in Japanese that they say are not found in individual or ego-focused emotions, including:

> *fureai*—a feeling of connection with someone, *shitashimi*—feeling of familiarity with someone, *sonkei*—feeling of response for someone, *amae*—hopeful expectation of someone's indulgence and favor, *tanomi*—feeling of relying on someone, *oime*—feeling of indebtedness.[34]

All of these emotions arise out of specific relationships with others. In America, on the other hand, people view their emotions in terms of individual identity or what Markus and Kitayama call "ego-focused emotions." Some semanticists have described contemporary English as lacking in emotional depth. Wierzbicka, for example, argues that the word for "grief" in English used to carry a greater depth of feeling in the past and that the word "happy" has become more frequently mentioned as a catch-all for emotions:

> Thus, modern English has exorcised woes, sorrows and griefs (in the plural) from the fabric of normal life. At the same time, "happiness" has come to be seen as the stuff of everyday life, and the word happy has become one of the most widely used English emotion adjectives—perhaps even the most widely used one of all.[35]

English speakers show emotion in their facial expressions; Asians typically do not. Instead, Asian use other nonverbal behaviors, including eye movement, that also communicates.[36] Asian facial expressions are often perceived as emotionless.[37] Asians also respond in ways that are quite different than the way English speakers respond. In some situations Asians would respond with a happy face or a smile in situations in which English speakers would respond with guilt or embarrassment, such as when they arrive late for class.[38]

In order to understand the emotion of a person, Asians not only need to understand the dynamics of the social context, they also need the ability

34. Ibid., 239.
35. Wierzbicka, "Emotion and Culture," 583.
36. Rösch and Segler, "Communication with Japanese," 61.
37. Kim, "Expression of Emotions," 40.
38. Ibid., 41.

to read the emotional state of the other person. In Korean, *nunchi* is the ability to read a person's emotional state in order to know how to respond.[39] Japanese use what they call *kuuki* to get a sense of the atmosphere of the group in order to know how to respond appropriately.[40] Underlying one's emotional feeling is the history of social interaction based on *on* (debt in a relationship)[41] and *giri* (obligation to repay a debt in a relationship).[42] The ability to read other people's emotions and "face" is foundational to Strong Community cultures.[43] (See more on "face" in chapter 10.)

Asian languages also have additional words or parts of words that indicate honor or respect to those in higher status as well as words or parts of words that are "self-humbling."[44] Japanese and Korean are two languages that have the most developed system of honorifics.[45]

Some scholars note that English words tend to be more general than words in Chinese and other Asian languages. Palmer and Wu note that the word "break" in English does not require clarification of the action that caused the break or how the break occurred (split open, shattered, etc.).[46] When an English speaker describes a situation in which something broke, they do not have to supply additional information about the context, while in Asian languages the words themselves indicate not only how the break was made (splinters, pieces, etc.) but also what the result of the break looked like (shattered, in a line, irregularly shaped, etc.).[47] This means that English speakers may not be giving enough information to Asian language speakers when they try to communicate. Zhang and Baker conclude that English speakers listen to the content of what is being said while Asian speakers listen for how something is described and said.[48] English phrases also use directional prepositions such as "up, down, in, out, and of" to create metaphors for different meanings. However, in Japanese and other

---

39. Ibid., 42.

40. Ito, "Socio-Cultural Backgrounds," 117.

41. Wierzbicka, "Japanese Key Words," 359.

42. Ibid., 366.

43. Kim and Nam, "Concept and Dynamics of Face," 525.

44. Brown, "Contrasts Between Korean and Japanese Honorifics," 379.

45. Ibid., 378.

46. Palmer and Wu, "Verb Semantics," 68.

47. Ibid., 66.

48. Zhang and Baker, *Inside the Chinese Mind*, 470.

Asian languages these ideas are contained within the verbs themselves.[49] When English speakers talk to speakers of Asian languages there is much information about a situation that is not translated, as well as cultural practices that contribute to much misunderstanding.

Word Order

Japanese and Korean belong to the same language family[50] and have many similarities in grammar, word meanings, and sounds. The two languages also have the same basic word order in transitive clauses: Subject-Object-Verb (SOV).[51] The word order can vary, but the verb typically comes at the end.[52] Japanese and Korean can also mark word order with an additional particle on the noun and the verb.[53] The nouns are marked by their grammatical role in the sentence, by the focus of the sentence, as well as by number.[54] Japanese and Korean also include honorifics, tense, mood, and connection to the overall topic of the conversation.[55]

According to Yang, Chinese has a Subject-Verb-Object (SVO) word order similar to English, but also has a more complicated word system that describes actions more precisely than English.[56]

Japanese allows many Subjects to be dropped, and Korean also allows the Subject to be dropped if it is understood from the context. Chinese allows some Subject-less clauses, although not as often as Japanese or Korean. On the other hand, English requires that a Subject be expressed in complete clauses, and even creates a "dummy" Subject if there is no Subject, as in "It is raining" and "There are difficulties."

With the verb at the end of sentences in Japanese and Korean the most important part of the sentence is not given until the end. Coleman notes that this also encourages people not to talk until the other person has

---

49. Yasuda, "Learning Phrasal Words," 251.

50. Georg et al., "Telling General Linguists about Altaic," 73–74.

51. Sohn, "State of the Art," 35. About 45 percent of the world's languages have SOV (Subject-Object-Verb) word order and 42 percent use SVO (Subject-Verb-Object).

52. Hwang, *Discourse Features*, 6.

53. Cho and Sells, "Lexical Account," 142.

54. Ibid., 142.

55. Ibid., 120.

56. Yang, "Parameter," 384.

finished speaking, unlike English speakers who do not have to wait for the other person to stop talking before they start talking.[57]

Writing systems

Another difference between the three Asian languages we are discussing and English is how the languages are written. Japanese, Korean (at least in part), and Chinese use a character writing system.[58] Japanese has three writing systems: two syllabary writing systems (*hiragana* and *katagana*) in which a symbol represents a syllable, as well as a character writing system (*kanji*) in which a character represents a unit of meaning, a word, or a combined meaning unit. Korean uses an alphabetic system (*hangul*) as its primary method of writing, but also uses characters (*hanja*) for some words. Japanese and Korean both use some Chinese-based characters as a basic unit for writing. There are about 50,000 characters in the Chinese system, although only 7,000 are generally used. Chinese words typically have two characters representing two syllables. Knowing the two characters does not always lead to understanding the meaning of the combined characters, however. English does not use a character-based writing system. The basic unit in English is the letter, and words can easily be understood by reading the combination of letters. In contrast to Asian languages, English uses letters to form words rather than characters to form concepts. Learning to read and write Asian languages, therefore, is more complex than learning to read and write English.[59]

Use of Questions

When English speakers ask a question, they normally expect a straightforward response or answer to their question. However, the questions that hierarchical Asians ask are more often a command. For example, if a senior pastor asks an English Ministry (EM) pastor if he would like to attend early morning prayer, the senior pastor does not expect an answer. He expects the EM pastor to attend early morning prayer. When the EM pastor responds

57. Coleman, "Teaching Culture," 330.
58. Daniels and Bright, *World's Writing Systems*, 4.
59. Schmitt et al., "Language," 419–31.

with a "no" this response can cause the senior pastor to lose face because his request is not fulfilled as expected in a Hierarching culture.

English speakers also expect to receive a clear "yes" or "no" from a yes/no question. However, when English speakers speak to Asians (Chinese, Japanese, Koreans) they often find it difficult to determine if their "yes" really means "yes" or whether it actually means "no." Japanese tend to avoid "yes" or "no" responses fearing confrontation because confrontation indicates a lack of harmony.[60] This is also similar in Chinese where people avoid a "yes" or "no" answer in order to save face, either one's own face or another person's.[61] Korean language speakers also need to determine whether or not a "yes" or a "no" will be face threatening. If so, they use various words to soften the "no," such as hesitations or excuses or self-devaluing comments about themselves.[62]

Untangling the Intersection of Culture

We've looked at some of the challenges that occur at the intersection of Individuating (Americanized Asians) and Hierarching (Asianized Americans) cultures that are reinforced by differences in language structure. In using the Structure and Community theory of culture, a person's Culture-based Judging System (CbJS) responses identify their cultural explanations. For example, when the older Asianized Americans' requests to a younger person are not fulfilled, they can become frustrated, upset, or angry, showing that their CbJS has been violated. On the other hand, younger Americanized Asians can become frustrated, upset, or angry at requests from older people because they were not given the opportunity to make an individual choice whether to obey or disobey the request. When both sides are operating from their own cultural perspective, it is impossible to find a satisfactory or biblical solution to the misunderstandings that occur.

A better solution would be for both sides to understand the cultural differences and to ask God for help in identifying their CbJS responses to cultural differences and to ask for God's wisdom in resolving the misunderstandings. The next two chapters discuss the source of the Strong Structure of Asian culture based on Confucian thought (chapter 9) and the Strong

---

60. Rösch and Segler, "Communication with Japanese," 57.

61. Chang, "Harmony as Performance," 160.

62. Byon, "Teaching Refusals," 4.

Community features that come from Buddhist and Taoist thinking (chapter 10).

Reflection Questions

1. Describe a frustrating situation that included language differences between English and an Asian language.

2. How does knowing about language differences help you to think differently about the other person?

3. Meditate on Ps 133:1; Zech 6:13; Rom 12:16; and 1 Pet 3:8. Spend twenty minutes in prayer and write some thoughts based on what God is speaking to you about as a result of your reflective prayer.

9

Confucian Principles Foster Hierarchical Structure

AS WE SAW IN chapters 2 through 5, many Asian cultural values are very similar to biblical values, but are based on a different view of humanity. Confucianism considers that a human being becomes a person as they fulfill the social expectations of their role/s and thereby develop virtues.[1] When people fulfill their social roles, they shape the Strong Structure of Asian culture. Christians consider that human beings are made in God's image and as such have the potential to reflect God's virtuous character through his enabling and their trust in God. American Christians view Christianity as a personal faith and develop their own behavior based on their own beliefs. American Christians do not have a Strong Structure culture.

Asian cultures have been greatly influenced by many different schools of thought, including Confucian, Buddhist, and Taoist thinking. Although some of the thinking of one tradition may be contrary to the others, in the Asian context they exist in harmonious tension. That is, Confucian thinking provides the hierarchical structural distinctions and expectations for social behavior; Buddhism prioritizes reciprocity; and Taoism focuses on *wu wei* "doing nothing" that actually means doing things the Taoist way. Confucian social ethics shape Strong Structure, but also shape Strong Community through filial piety and ritual.

In this chapter we focus on the Strong Structure created by the five Confucian relationships that form the framework for proper behavior or *li* 禮 (knowing your role in life and acting accordingly) and the basic virtue of filial piety (caring for your parents as they cared for you). *Li* and filial piety

---

1. Weiming, "Ecological Turn," 256.

describe the expected behaviors of the Confucian five relationships that build Strong Community.

The Five Relationships of Confucianism and *Li*

The ancient Chinese viewed Heaven and Earth as parents of all things. The order of things began with Heaven and Earth, and from them came male and female[2] and from them came husband and wife, then children and the distinction between ruler and subject and older and younger. When these distinctions are observed, the appropriate and right behavior for each role can be established. The *I-Ching* explains:

> Heaven and earth existing, all (material) things then got their existence. All (material) things having existence, afterwards there came male and female. From the existence of male and female there came afterwards husband and wife. From husband and wife there came father and son. From father and son there came ruler and minister. From ruler and minister there came high and low. When (the distinction of) high and low had existence, afterwards came the arrangements of propriety and righteousness.[3]

These social roles are learned within the family and then extended to society with the main responsibility for this learning on the head (of the State as well as the family).[4] The ideal person finds identity in family relationships, rather than as an individual alone, through internalizing the social values developed through these relationships. Weiming notes:

> [S]ociety is not conceived of as something out there that is being imposed on the individual. It is in essence an extended self. The internalization of social values . . . can therefore be interpreted as a creative step taken by the self to enter into human relatedness for the sake of none other than its own realization.[5]

Around 500 BC there was much political turmoil in China. The political leaders were corrupt, and society as a whole was full of chaos and disorder.

2. Male and female from the Western perspective is an either/or and contradictory dichotomy, but in the Eastern perspective male and female are complementing and fulfilling. Li-Hsiang, *Confucianism and Women*, 49.

3. *I-Ching*, 31–32.

4. Lai, "*Confucian Moral Thinking*," 251.

5. Weiming, "Li," 25.

Confucius attributed this disorder to the lack of propriety (*li*) on the part of the rulers. If rulers fulfilled their roles appropriately and conducted themselves properly, Confucius believed, society would become more orderly and good.[6] This could be accomplished if leaders in particular set the example by following the proper order of relationships and by behaving according to their role or doing things the right way (*tao* or *dao* 濤). If leaders did not do the right thing there would be chaos and rebellion rather than good government. Lan summarizes this principle:

> They are without the rules of proper conduct and justice (*yi*), so there is rebellion, disorder, and no good government. In ancient times the sage kings knew that human nature is evil, selfish, vicious, unrighteous, rebellious, and of itself could not bring about good government. For this reason they created the rules of proper conduct (*li*) and justice (*yi*). They established laws and ordinances to force and beautify the natural feelings of humans, thus rectifying them. They trained to obedience and civilized humans' natural feelings, thus guiding them. Then good government arose and humans followed the right way (*tao*).[7]

Li is the true expression of what it means to be human or how humans are to interact with each other. *Li* is not just appropriately performing a social role, but also knowing the appropriate behavior expected of one's role in various social contexts. The performance of *li* is learned over time and forms habits that become ritual ways of doing things that are considered to clean a person from biological impurities. As Herr explains:

> *Li* is the civilized expression of human impulse, and human desires and needs are processed through *li* and cleansed of biological impurities. Through *li*, interactions between people become ritualistic and aesthetic and one step removed from direct expressions of raw emotion. As such, adherence to *li* does not come naturally to ordinary people. Novices must go through years of inculcation and habituation to be finally able to internalize *li* and make it their second nature.[8]

Confucius proposed that *li* should be learned through the social interactions within the five hierarchical relationships (ruler to subject, parent to child, husband to wife, older to younger, and friend to friend) that not only

6. Yao, "Confucius," 20–33.

7. Lan, *History of Chinese Philosophy*, 294.

8. Herr, "Is Confucianism Compatible?," 477–78.

follow the natural order of the universe but also lead to social order. Even in friendships age determines which friend has a higher status than the other.[9]

Within these five relationships ten virtues / types of righteousness and justice are developed: benevolence (ruler) and loyalty (subject), kindness (father) and filial duty (son), gentleness (elder brother) and obedience (younger brother), righteousness (husband) and submission (wife), kindness (older friend) and deference (younger friend).

> What are the things which humans consider righteous (*yi*)? Kindness on the part of the father, and filial duty on that of the son; gentleness on the part of the elder brother, and obedience on that of the younger; righteousness on the part of the husband, and submission on that of the wife; kindness on the part of the elders, and deference on that of juniors; benevolence on the part of the ruler, and loyalty on that of the minister. These are the ten things which humans consider being right.[10]

The goal of propriety (*li*) in these relationships is to develop virtues (*yi*) that can establish an orderly society. That is, these virtues develop one's inner character by repeatedly fulfilling one's duty in accordance with each social role. Social relationships are not just a name or label for a social role, but also the values developed from the responsibilities and expectations of that role. Cheng explains:

> Names for Confucius were not merely labels for things in nature, but also include labels for the relationships between individuals and the values inherent in those relationships . . . Thus it is clear that, for Confucius, labels denoting social positions and ethical relationships are also names.[11]

The five Confucian relationships are understood to be based on "heaven's ordinance," and the virtues are developed through mutual and reciprocal obligations that uphold the hierarchical distinctions based on family relationships. The hierarchical distinctions also influence how one loves others according to their place in the hierarchy. Cheng says that the distinctions:

> . . . are mutually and reciprocally obligated, prescribing a basic sense of social hierarchy. They provide a model for social behavior

9. Yao, "Confucius," 20–33.

10. Hwang, "Chinese Relationalism," 170.

11. Cheng, *New Dimensions*, 222.

based on familial relations. In Confucianism, then, man's love of others is hierarchically graded and is conditioned by this framework "in accordance with heaven's ordinance."[12]

Confucian Relationships and Scripture

Although many Confucian practices are similar to those found in Scripture, Asian cultural practices can easily be interpreted through Confucian eyes rather than through God's eyes. For example, there are commands to obey and submit to those in authority, but we easily overlook the rest of the verses that explain *how* we are to obey and submit—*as unto the Lord*.

Scripture commands us to obey and submit to authority figures (Rom 13:1, 5; Heb 13:17; 1 Pet 2:13; Titus 3:1). We are to submit to leaders because God has put them in authority (Rom 13:1); because of the potential punishment and because of our conscience (Rom 13:7); and, because leaders take care of us, we should make their work a joy instead of a burden (Heb 13:17). Jesus told his disciples not to be like the Gentiles leaders, who lord it over others even though they call themselves "Benefactors" (Luke 22:25–26).

Children are also commanded to obey and honor their parents (Deut 21:18) because it is right (Eph 6:1) and it pleases God (Col 3:20). Children are also to honor their parents so that they can live long in the land (Exod 20:12; Deut 5:16; Matt 15:4). Anyone who curses his father and mother should be put to death (Mark 7:10). Fathers are not to exasperate their children (Eph 6:4).

Wives are instructed to submit to their husbands (Eph 5:22–24; Col 3:18) as they would submit to Christ. Additionally, each person should submit to others out of reverence for Christ (Eph 5:21). The basis of this submission is submission to God and his law (2 Chr 30:8; Job 22:21). A wife is to submit to her husband so that he might be won over by her testimony (1 Pet 3:1). A husband is to love his wife to make her holy and blameless as Christ loved the church and gave his life for it (Eph 5:25–27).

In Titus leaders are commanded to train older men and women so that they in turn can help the younger men and women. The older men should be "sober-minded, dignified, self-controlled, sound in faith, in love, and in steadfastness" (Titus 2:2). The older women are to be "be reverent in behavior, not slanderers or slaves to much wine." They are to teach what

12. Ibid., 209.

is good (Titus 2:3). Then the older women can train the younger women to love their husbands and children and to be pure, kind, self-controlled, and submissive to their husbands so that God's word will not be maligned (Titus 2:3–5).

A friend is one who loves at all times (Prov 17:17), helps you when you fall (Eccl 4:10), and one who gives their life for you (John 15:13).

Confucian Filial Piety

Filial piety is the foundational virtue of Confucianism. By fulfilling the expected social responsibilities (*li*) to care for one's parents, a child learns to repay his parents for the care they first extended to him. If this practice is learned well in the home, it can be extended to others in society, especially to those in authority or to those higher in status.

Based on the love and care their parents gave them, children learn how to take care of their parents when they get old. Because Asian parents have spent a lot of time and energy to ensure the success of their children, they anticipate that their children will care for them in the same manner when they are old. Lai explains:

> The starting point of filial piety is actually the responsibility of parents to demonstrate to their children the concern and love appropriate to the parent-child relationship. It is to these demonstrated qualities that the children appropriately respond.[13]

The son[14] (and his wife) are expected to fulfill the son's filial responsibilities with a demeanor that shows pleasure in order to put his parents at ease. Their actions should not appear to be a heavy obligation. *The Book of Rites* says, "Care for parents should not be a tiresome obligation; the filial son and his wife will do it with an appearance of pleasure to make their parents feel at ease."[15]

The purpose of filial piety is to honor the name of the parents. If a child learns filial piety in the home, he is able to develop the virtues in the other relationships and that brings honor to the name of the parents.[16] *The Book of Filial Piety* states that ". . . to establish oneself, to enhance the

13. Lai, "Confucian Moral Thinking," 258.

14. The major responsibility of caring for parents often falls to the first son's wife.

15. *Book of Rites*, 2:1.

16. Hsu, "Confucianism," 61.

Way, and to leave a good reputation behind, in order to make one's parents illustrious, are the ultimate goal of filiality."[17]

Filial piety implies two important responsibilities for the child—one is the importance of the responsibility for their parents' care and the other is reciprocity for the care the parent gave the child. The idea of enduring intergenerational relationships is central to the meaning of filial piety.[18]

The written character for filial piety 孝 is the same in Chinese (*hsiao*), Japanese (*kou*), and Korean (*hyodo*). It is composed of two characters—an old man (*lao*) (indicating age) and a son or child (*zi*), depicting the son carrying the old man or father on his shoulders. According to Sure, "This illustrates the traditional relationship of youth to age."[19]

Filial piety is not only unquestioned obedience of the son to the father, the son must also "learn to suppress his own desires, anticipate the wishes of his father, and take his father's commands as sacred edicts."[20] This obedience is expected even if his parent has committed immoral acts. Children should still respond with unconditional filial piety by "conceal[ing] the misconduct" of parents.[21] Herr notes, "If parents do not mend their ways despite the children's efforts, children must never overstep what is prescribed by their filial duty while trying to lead parents in the right direction as best as they can."[22]

Because parents sacrifice a lot for a son in providing life and health, it is the duty of the son to repay his parents for their kindness and care to him. This includes not doing anything that would injure or hurt them. The son should also take care of himself so that he can fulfill his filial role. *The Book of Filial Piety* states:

> Now filial piety is the root of (all) virtue, and (the stem) out of which grows (all moral) teaching . . . Our bodies—to every hair and bit of skin—are received by us from our parents, and we must not presume to injure or wound them. This is the beginning of filial piety.[23]

---

17. Cited in Li, "Shifting Perspectives," 230.
18. Ho, "Filial Piety," 349.
19. Sure, "Filial Respect," 59.
20. Weiming, "Selfhood," 234.
21. *Analects* XIII:18.
22. Herr, "Is Confucianism Compatible?," 473.
23. *Book of Filial Piety*.

The extent of filial piety in China is such that the law requires children to care for their elderly parents or face legal punishment.[24] The most serious thing that can happen in a person's life is to be disowned by their parents, thus losing their family ties.[25]

Filial piety demonstrates the strength of family relationships. A son is filial if he follows in his father's footsteps. That is, if the father can be seen through the actions of his son, the son is filial. In fact, it is more important to reflect your father than to do the right thing. *The Analects* explain:

> A son is filial only if he does not change from his father's way after 3 years. A son is not filial if he changes from his father's way after 3 years even if his conduct is good.[26]

The Analects also note that there is no greater love than to show love to one's parents by repaying them (reciprocity *shu* 恕) for their previous care.[27] A son cares for his father in the way he would want his son to treat him. This concept of reciprocity is reflected in the Confucian Golden Rule, "Do not do to others what you would not have them do to you."[28]

There are five main duties of a filial son: 1) support one's parents in daily life, 2) honor/revere/obey one's parents, 3) produce male heirs, 4) give honor to ancestors, and 5) mourn and offer a memorial service and sacrifice after death.[29]

First, a son can support or care for his parents in daily life by providing things that lead to a healthy mind and body, making them happy and comfortable. Sung elaborates:

> . . . care and services for an elder's mind and body, e.g., providing personal care, nourishment, homemaking and health and social services; making them feel happy and comfortable.[30]

Care respect[31] is providing care and services as a means of showing respect. There are several types of care respect that can be shown: victual respect (serving parents the foods and drinks of their choice), gift respect (giving

24. "Elderly Protection Law."
25. Tseng, *Asian Culture*, 5.
26. *Analects* I:11.
27. *Analects* XII:2.
28. *Analects*, XV:23.
29. Li, "Shifting Perspectives," 221.
30. Sung, "Elder Respect," 20.
31. Ibid., 20.

them gifts of things they like), and care respect as in caring for parents when they are sick. When parents are cared for in one or more of these ways on a regular basis, they feel appropriately reciprocated and honored. If they are not cared for in one or more of these ways, parents may think their child doesn't love them and is not grateful for the things they did for the child. In the same way, older Asians, and males in particular, will also feel reciprocated and honored if those under them show care respect for the services they provide in their role as a leader of the church or community. If they are not reciprocated or shown care in one of these ways from time to time, they may also think that they are either not doing enough to care for those under them or that the people who are under them are not thankful for what they provide. The leader may then feel justified in reprimanding or punishing those under him to balance out the lack of reciprocation.

Secondly, a son honors, reveres, and obeys his parents through linguistic respect by using respectful language when speaking to them; salutary respect by greeting elders with an appropriate bow; presentational respect by having a pleasant demeanor; spatial respect by providing elders and parents with honorable seats or places; celebrative respect by celebrating the birthdays of elders; public respect by bowing and giving preference to elders in public; acquiescent respect by being obedient by acquiescing to elders; and precedential respect by giving preferential treatment to elders.[32]

If parents are shown respect on a regular basis, they feel honored and reciprocated. In the same way older Asians will feel honored and appropriately reciprocated if younger Asians demonstrate respect to them. Conversely, if their parents are not shown respect, they feel they have not been reciprocated appropriately nor honored appropriately, and something bad may happen. It is considered the responsibility of the older person to correct or discipline a younger person who does not show appropriate honor to their parents and elders.

Thirdly, a son is filial by producing a male heir to carry on the family name. The Chinese philosopher Mencius said, "There are three ways of being unfilial, and to have no heir is the greatest of them."[33] Having a male heir is very important because this is how the family name is perpetuated. Having a female heir does not enable the family name to be carried on. Older women continually ask unmarried men and women when they are going to get married. Older people ask childless married couples when

32. Ibid., 21.
33. *Mencius* 4A:26.

they will have children. Having a male child helps a son be filial as he has provided an heir to carry on the family name.

Although young unmarried Asians may not know the cultural reason their parents and older people continually ask them about their single marital status, they are often bothered by the frequency with which they are asked. They often don't understand how important it is for their parents to be assured of a male heir and to maintain the reputation within their social group. Asian parents want their children to fulfill their role in providing an heir to carry on their family name.

Fourthly, the filial son gives honor and respect to his ancestors by involving them in his everyday life. Just as filial piety is the basic value of Confucian thinking, remembering or worshipping ancestors is the basic value of filial piety.[34] A son is filial by doing well in life, having a good reputation, and bringing honor to the family name. He joins in the various ritual ceremonies that give honor to his ancestors, asks them for advice, protection, success, and guidance. He also keeps the family genealogy, thereby bringing honor to the family name.

The Chinese consider ancestor worship to be mainly about commemorating one's origin and the source of their life. It is also a way of repaying the debt that one owes for the things they have in life. There is also a sense of blessing coming from repaying one's debt.[35] Dickson explains that in Japan some ways in which respect or reverence is shown to the dead is by bowing, burning incense, serving favorite food, pressing palms together, observing memorial days, and addressing the dead at the funeral and at the gravesite.[36] Yang adds that a filial Chinese will wear white clothing, wail, burn paper money, make offerings, and set up ancestral tablets.[37] In Korea a spirit throne where the ancestor lives during the mourning period is constructed, a funeral song is sung, and daily portions of the meal are set aside for the departed. Guests also come and bow before the deceased as they would a living person. In many ways the funeral rituals are a means of extending the life of the deceased person but also of repaying them for their care during their lifetime.[38]

---

34. Dickson, "Protestant Perspectives," 43.

35. Hsieh, "Filial Piety," 180.

36. Dickson, "Protestant Perspectives," 48.

37. Yang, *Chinese Christians*, 140.

38. Yim, "Psychocultural Features," 166.

The Asian view of the person is not only a group identity with other living family members; it also includes the dead as well as the living. Day-to-day activities include interactions between the living and the dead. The deceased are asked to protect, advise, and participate in daily activities. Dickson notes that in Japan, Christians believe that showing reverence to the ancestors is no different than showing reverence to the living.[39]

Fifthly, after their parents' death, the children are obligated to mourn, offer a memorial service, and give a sacrifice. It is very important to be at the deathbed of one's parents. It is also the custom for the oldest Chinese son to close the eyes of his parents when they die. Lin explains:

> The greatest regret a Chinese gentleman could have was the eternally lost opportunity of serving his old parents with medicine and soup on their deathbed, or not to be present when they died.[40]

A number of rituals in the Chinese funeral must be observed in the appropriate way. Wolf outlines a number of the important steps. A geomancer is called to determine the right time to place the body in the coffin. Then five nails are driven into the coffin while a chant invokes prosperity for the descendants. A priest is called to help the deceased travel through difficult places on his journey to the place of the dead and the family makes offerings to the dead on the seventh, fourteenth, twenty-first, and twenty-eighth day. The underlying reason for honoring ancestors is the belief that the dead can come back to cause trouble if they are not cared for appropriately.[41] A filial son or daughter should mourn for three years as was modeled by Confucius's followers.

The honoring or worshipping of ancestors is probably the most challenging cultural practice that Asian Christians face. Some Asian churches have substituted other rituals for honoring rather than worshiping ancestors. One of the earliest recorded substitutions was in Korea in the mid-1890s when a Korean church developed a Christian substitute for their grieving ritual. The event, called *chu'do yebae*, was an opportunity for Christians to give thanks to God for the life of the deceased person and served as a substitute for the *chesa* ritual.[42] Dickson says that Christianization of ancestor worship in Japan has not been successful organizationally,

---

39. Dickson, "Protestant Perspectives," 46.
40. Lin, "Growing Old," 190–99.
41. Wolf, *Religion and Ritual*, 60.
42. Grayson, "Kwallye Samga," 128.

but Japanese Christians have developed their own ways of honoring their ancestors.[43]

Confucian Filial Piety and Scripture

The Confucian virtue of filial piety is similar to scriptural teaching. Asians who are trained from childhood to be respectful to parents have a good model for learning how God desires them to respect and honor their parents and other older people. Scripture also places a high value on the family and on love and care of one another. Lai notes:

> A commendable aspect of Confucian thought in this respect is its emphasis on family values and its attempt to reach back to the family as the source of moral affection and, hence, of ways of caring for others.[44]

Although filial piety is commanded in Scripture, the reason for being filial is different from that presented in Confucian philosophy. The Christian honors his parents because it is right and pleases God, while the Confucian honors his family out of duty to the family and society.

> Children obey your parents in the Lord, *for this is right.* (Eph 6:1)

> Children obey your parents in everything, *for this pleases the Lord.* (Col 3:20)

However, Scripture does not limit care just for parents but extends care to all family members. Care for family members is a sign of one's faith.

> But if anyone does not provide for his relatives, and especially for members of his household, he has *denied the faith* and is worse than an unbeliever. (1 Tim 5:8)

Although Scripture supports honor of parents, it does not condone worshipping anyone but God (Exod 34:14). God is the one who deserves honor (Eccl 6:2; Ps 84:11). If we need guidance and wisdom, God gives it to us (Jas 1:5).

Scripture also contains examples of children being filial to their parents. Solomon showed respect to his mother by bowing down to her and providing her a special seat (1 Kgs 2:19). Jesus was respectful to his parents

---

43. Dickson, "Protestant Perspectives," 57.

44. Lai, "Confucian Moral Thinking," 267.

(Luke 2:51). In the Old Testament there was severe punishment for the child who did not obey his parents (Deut 21:18–21).

A Christian is filial because he is made in God's image and desires to become what God intended him to be. This includes not only being filial to his parents but also showing respect to other family members of the faith. The Christian is also commanded to treat each person without differentiation (Gal 3:28) and to be subject to others out of reverence for Christ (Eph 5:21).

Although the Confucian value of filial piety is the basis for the social functioning of the Asian family and looks similar to practices found in Scripture, it differs in fundamental ways. Followers of Confucianism idolize the family and the social relationships that suppress individuals made in God's image. Confucian values contribute to a sense of duty without an underlying positive motivation and can lead to bitterness. Scripture views all people as equally made in God's image. It is crucial for Asian believers to examine and understand Asian cultural values in light of Scripture and to recognize how these cultural values can reflect or distort God's truth and can prevent them from experiencing the grace of God.

Reflection Questions

Reflect on the following questions about Confucianism. Share your thoughts with others and get their input.

1. In what ways do you see Confucian relationships, propriety, and filial piety at work in your life and ministry?

2. How do you feel about the Confucian expectations that others place on you?

3. Spend twenty minutes or so prayerfully reflecting on the information presented in this chapter. Ask God to show you how he wants you to address the Confucian values that impact your life and ministry.

10

Buddhist and Taoist Principles Foster Reciprocity

THIS CHAPTER BUILDS ON the Confucian ideal of benevolence or care of the community[1] to show how Buddhist reciprocity and Taoist yin-yang harmony maintain Strong Community values.

People in Strong Community cultures have a strong sense of social responsibility for those in their group. This is a major responsibility of those who are older to take care of those who are younger. In Asian cultures the concept of care is seen in the Chinese word *ren* 仁 translated as "benevolence" but also as "humanness" or "to be a person one has to care for others."[2] The meaning of *ren* is closely connected with *li*, that is, benevolence is expressed according to one's role. Fulfilling one's role is believed to internalize benevolence or care over time. Asian American immigrants are drawn to Asian American churches because they can find *ren* in a social context where they can speak their own language and follow their own customs, and also receive help finding a job, a place to live, and advice about how to go about daily activities.

People in Strong Community cultures take care of each other because their identity comes from belonging to the group. Taking care of each other is reciprocal. The person in the higher position (ruler, husband, parent, older, friend) is expected to care for those in the lower position, but others are also expected to care for one another. When a person receives from and gives care to others they develop a sense of loyalty and submission. This care is not only in the provision of material needs but also in the social

1. Additional details about this chapter can be found in "Caring for Community: Asian Face-Saving" presented by Sheryl Takagi Silzer at the Evangelical Theological Society conference in Milwaukee, WI, November 15, 2012.

2. Li, *"Confucian Concept of Jen,"* 74.

need for leaders or higher-status people to be perceived as fulfilling their benevolent role. If they do not fulfill their role appropriately, not only their reputation but also the reputation of the group as a whole can be damaged. In the same manner, a person in a lower position can make a person in a higher position look bad by not submitting or showing respect or loyalty to the leader or person in the higher position. When a person does not perform according to the expectations of their social role, it results in shame for the individual and the group. This then requires "facework" in which group members help restore and maintain the group's reputation.

Taking Care of the Community through Facework

Asians care for each other through the cultural custom of "facework"—maintaining the group's reputation. It is very important to care physically, emotionally, and spiritually for one another, but also to uphold the reputation of the group. Persons says that face involves two main aspects: "1) a person's claim to value—a (usually) positive presentation of one's self into social space and 2) face value awarded or legitimized by others."[3]

Asian face arises from the sense of indebtedness that a person has from birth. In Japanese this indebtedness is called *on* and includes many kinds of obligations. The manner in which a person fulfills obligations is a demonstration of moral character. In Chinese this reciprocity (*shu* 恕) fosters relationships (*guanxi* 關係 or 关系) in which resources are shared and ties continue past one's lifetime into the next generation.

Within Confucian thinking a person's social role defines what and how the person reciprocates. The ruler protects and cares for those under him, and subjects reciprocate by showing respect and by fulfilling the ruler's requests. Husbands provide support for their wives and children, and in return wives and children reciprocate with submission and obedience. As we saw in the previous chapter, children are also expected to reciprocate the care their parents gave them when they were young by caring for their parents when they are old. When each person fulfills the expectations of their social role, ideally peace and harmony of the family and society results, and group face is maintained.

Asians fulfill their social role through the use of "face" in their relationships with their family and community, as it is a means of gaining honor and avoiding shame. The hierarchical structure provides the context

3. Persons, *Face Dynamics*, 16.

for "face." Face is a concept that affects every part of Asian social life[4] and includes one's "appearance and look, as indicator of emotion and character, as focus of interaction and relationship, and as locus of dignity and prestige."[5] Face is so important that it is relevant to any social interaction. Ho states that face is:

> . . . the respectability and/or deference that a person can claim for him/herself from others, by virtue of the relative position he occupies in the social network and the degree to which he is judged to have functioned adequately in the position as well as acceptably in his social conduct.[6]

Face has also been described as a social interpersonal commodity that as a resource can be "threatened, enhanced, maintained, and bargained over."[7] Asians, as members of a strong group or community, are concerned about how others view them, and this concern motivates them to behave in a manner that is acceptable to the other people in the community. By taking care of others, one also takes care of oneself.[8]

There are a number of words in Asian cultures that refer to face and how to maintain it. In Chinese the two words for face that work together are *lian* and *mianzi* (or *mientze*). *Lian* 脸 refers to "the confidence of society in the integrity of ego's moral character."[9] By fulfilling the expectation of their social roles and their potential as human beings, people gain the confidence of society. A person can lose *lian* by acting in a socially unacceptable or immoral way. This loss of face affects not only the person; his whole family loses face, and face is difficult to restore.[10] *Mianzi* 面子 is social capital gained through "reputation achieved through getting along in life through success and ostentation."[11] Social capital is gained through relationships that enable a person to obtain resources. Hwang notes, "Within a social network, having *mientze* enhances not only social position but also many kinds of privileges that further improve the quality of life."[12]

4. Ho, "On the Concept of Face," 872.

5. Yu, "What Does our Face Mean to us?," 151.

6. Ho, "On the Concept of Face," 883.

7. Oetze et al., "Analysis," 384.

8. Persons, *Face Dynamics*, 2.

9. Hu, "Chinese Concepts of Face," 45.

10. Ibid., 50.

11. Ibid., 45.

12. Hwang, "Face and Favor," 961.

In Japanese the word *kao* (顔 かお) refers to face, features, or looks. In Korean *gibun* (기분) refers to a person's state of mind or feelings which need to be protected and *nunchi* (눈치) refers to the ability to judge or gauge another person's feelings. Several words are used in Korean to refer to face in a negative way (*nattsak, sangpandeki,* and *ssangtong*), while *yong-an* and *jo* refer to deference to face.[13]

In Japanese *aite no kimochi wo yomu* (相手の気持ちを読む) means reading the other person's mind and *haragei* (腹芸) "belly art" refers to a type of indirect communication that uses implications rather than straight-forward speech due to sensitivity to the other person's emotional state.[14]

Asian face is also a means of communicating, and "face reading" is an important part of life. The frequent use of the word "face" reveals its importance. Kim Kun-Ok gives the following examples from the Korean language:

> 'My face is wrinkled' means I am ashamed or discredited; 'You have smeared my face with black ink' means you have disgraced my dignity; 'His face is wide' means he has many influential friends; and 'one has no face to see' means he is very sorry for what has happened. 'His face is even or smooth' means he is nice-looking in a derogatory way; and 'My face itches' is used in a context in which a person receives an exaggerated compliment or service. In case a person does not meet another's expectation, he is often referred to being a person 'not worth even his face value.' To indicate an impudent person, 'he has thick facial skin' or 'even a weasel has a face' is frequently used. An imprudent person naturally has 'thin facial skin.'[15]

Giving face protects a relationship and includes actions that make a person look better in public or prevent them from looking worse.[16] Fulfilling the appropriate behaviors of one's social role within the five main relationships (subject to ruler, child to parent, wife to husband, younger to older, friend to friend) is the means for giving face. In an ideal world where everyone fulfills social expectations, the anticipated result is social harmony and a positive face or a good reputation of the group. Mitchell explains:

13. Kim, "What is Behind 'Face Saving'?," 2.

14. Rösch and Segler, "Communication," 61.

15. Kim, "What is Behind 'Face-Saving'?," 1–2. There are similar phrases in Chinese, Japanese, and other Asian languages.

16. Haugh and Hinze, "Metalinguistic Approach," 1593.

The value placed on giving or saving face is closely linked to the powerful theme of preservation of group harmony in Confucian societies as well as deep respect for the existing social order.[17]

However, we do not live in an ideal world, and some people may react negatively to the expectations of their social role, use their position to get more resources, or do things to enhance their own social standing. When people do not act according to the expectations of their social role, the group is shamed and face is lost. Fairbank notes that: "'Loss of face' is the loss of social approval through failure to observe the recognized rules of conduct."[18]

When face is lost, facework is required. Asian facework is the "artful process of diffusing and managing self-focused emotions and other-focused emotions."[19] Facework refers to strategies that Asians use to maintain, protect, support their reputation, or challenge another's place in the hierarchy, particularly when one has lost face.[20] These strategies give or restore face and are how Asians care for those in their community by maintaining the reputation of the group.

Higher-status people care for lower-status people by sharing or distributing resources.[21] The lower-status person can protect the relationship by showing respect to the higher-status person by addressing him with the appropriate title and by showing physical deference (e.g., by bowing) or doing what they ask. Giving face protects the relationship. Lower-status people give face when they attend to the feelings and emotions of higher-status people.

When a higher-status person is not treated according to his social level (e.g., not addressed with the appropriate terms, not consulted on a major decision, not obeyed nor bowed to), he loses face and is shamed. A higher-status person can also lose face if someone younger receives more social standing than he does. Face is also lost when a wife does not submit to her husband or when a child does not show respect to his parents (e.g., does not get good grades or get into good schools, does not make enough money, or does not have a male heir, etc.). Losing face means losing social approval and is also viewed as a threat to the social order because it not only

17. Mitchell, *Short Example*, 142.
18. Fairbank, *United States and China*, 104.
19. Ting-Toomey, "Face and Facework," 4.
20. Oetzel, "Typology of Facework," 400.
21. Hwang, "Chinese Relationalism," 174.

discredits one's social position, but also causes the group as a whole to be discredited. Mitchell explains:

> To cause someone to lose face is seen as a challenge to their position within the hierarchy—and thus a threat to the group order. If an Asian loses face it is equal to being socially discredited, he or she may no longer function effectively in the community. To lose face is very shameful.[22]

When face has been lost, a number of things can be done to save or restore face. For example, a child who received poor grades can save his parents' face by improving his grades. A son can enhance his parents' face by getting into a good school, making more money, or getting married and having a son. A younger person can save the face of an older person by asking forgiveness from the older person for doing things that caused them loss of face. Young people can give face by attending to the other person's emotions and fulfilling the expectations of their social role, such as agreeing with them or doing what they ask. They can also give face by helping with chores around the house, church, or ministry or just spending time with older people as a means of maintaining or enhancing their social credit. If a younger person doesn't act in the appropriate and expected manner, an older person is perceived to be justified in getting upset emotionally and physically punishing the younger person, even though the younger person is considered an adult (e.g., has graduated from college, is married, has children) in American culture.

Facework is also proactive. That is, one can do a number of things to give face in order to save face in the future. Showing respect to parents and older people, giving them gifts, and providing for their needs can become social capital that can be used when a person has a future need, such as money for school or other expenses, a decision that might previously be contrary to the older person's desires, etc.

Asian facework activities protect and maintain the social reputation of the family or society within the five Confucian relationships. The purpose of facework is to achieve social harmony by developing sensitivity for others, e.g., how they are feeling, what they are thinking, what they need, etc. This sensitivity is reciprocated and thereby maintains care for others in the group.

---

22. Mitchell, *Short Example*, 143.

Caring for One Another

Although Scripture does not endorse such a rigid hierarchy of relationships, it does command care and respect for others no matter the social position or circumstances (Phil 4:11). Although we have briefly looked at the honor shame dynamic in chapter 2 and seen how the honor and shame dynamic is typical of Strong Community, the focus in Scripture is on the behaviors that come from the heart because Christ has set the example (John 13:15). Based on our relationship with Christ, various virtues develop (e.g., kindness [Eph 4:32], filial duty [Eph 6:1], gentleness, [Gal 5:22], obedience and righteousness [Rom 2:13], submission and loyalty [Phil 4:3]).

In addition to submitting to authority figures and honoring our parents so that we may live long (Exod 20:12; Deut 5:16), we are also commanded to take care of the needs of family members (2 Tim 5:8). Believers do this by attending to one another's feelings and needs as a means of showing acceptance and love, as well as providing for them materially. The phrase "one another" implies reciprocity. We are commanded to accept one another just as Christ accepted us for the purpose of bringing praise to God (Rom 15:7). We are also to love one another deeply from our heart (1 Pet 1:22), just as Christ loved us (John 13:34). Because love comes from God, his love lives in us and is made complete in us (1 John 4:7). We are to be devoted to one another in brotherly love (Rom 12:10), serve one another in love (Gal 5:13), be kind and forgiving to one another (Eph 4:32), encourage and build each other up (1 Thess 5:11), and stimulate each other to love and good works (Heb 10:24). If we love each other we will be united in mind and thought (1 Cor 1:10), live in harmony (Rom 12:16), and be sympathetic, compassionate, and humble (1 Pet 3:8). As believers, we are commanded to seek God's face (Ps 105:4). When we look to him our faces are radiant and not covered with shame (Ps 34:4–5).

Buddhist Reciprocity[23]

Buddhist beliefs also reinforce Strong Community values. Buddhists believe that a person is not an isolated individual but an integral part of creation that is also interdependent;[24] that is, what happens to one part of

23. For additional information on this topic, see Silzer, "How Buddhist Spirituality Influences," 101–21.

24. Verhoeven, "Buddhist Ideas," 95.

creation, either person or thing, affects the world and others.[25] Therefore, a person's actions (*karma*) determine who they are today and what they might become in a future life.[26]

The main goal of Buddhism is to relieve human suffering by helping people to understand and address the causes of suffering.[27] This is accomplished through the Four Noble Truths: 1) Suffering (*dukkha*) is just a part of life and living (birth, illness, death, being separated from a loved one, etc.). 2) The cause of suffering comes from wanting the things that do not fulfill one's desires. 3) Wrong desires can be replaced by the right desire structure. 4) The right desire structure is to follow the Eightfold Path of Truth.[28] The Eightfold Path outlines the good deeds that enhance *karma* by gaining merit and purifying bad deeds.[29] The Eightfold Path is defined as: right understanding, right aspiration, right speech, right action, right livelihood, right effort, right mindfulness, and right concentration.

Examples of good deeds or good works that gain merit include joining and participating in the life of the Buddhist temple through sharing one's material resources with the monks, being a lay leader, and acting in a moral way.[30] Other good works include purchasing items or property for the temple as well as praying for the monks.[31] The good works in Buddhism can easily be compared similarly to good works in the Asian American church.

The Buddhist Strong Community view of the self requires reciprocity and thus, doing things for others can be interpreted as good works. The idea of gaining of merit through good works reinforces community ties through the reciprocal sharing of resources that also helps alleviate the suffering that is inherent in life.

Strong Community is also maintained by the Taoist belief of yin-yang harmony.

25. Bean, "In light of Anatman," 18, 24.
26. Humphreys, *Karma*, 12.
27. Bhagat, *Ancient Indian Asceticism*, 160.
28. Kishimoto, "Some Japanese Cultural Traits," 115.
29. Krishan, "Karma Vipaka," 205.
30. Adamek, "Impossibility of the Given," 136.
31. Walsh, "Economics of Salvation," 355.

Taoist Yin-Yang Harmony

Strong Community thinking is probably the most difficult concept for Weak Community cultures to understand. A case in point is Taoism/Daoism. Everything about Taoism is contrary to Weak Community thinking, which we saw in chapters 7 and 8. Weak Community (Individuating and Institutionalizing) cultures separate the physical from the spiritual using clearly defined categories with logical connections. On the other hand, Strong Community cultures (Hierarching and Interrelating) are more ambiguous and holistic where the spiritual and the physical, as well as humans and nature, are perceived to be integrated or together.

Strong Community starts with the universe and ties everything into it, both creation and humanity. This is one of the reasons why Taoism has been difficult to define in English. For the Chinese everything is related to the universe.[32] Ball explains that when *qi* or breath or vital energy separated, heaven and earth were born and the universe began.[33] Even the definition of *qi/chi* is difficult to express in English. Cunshan[34] tried to define it from several different disciplines (philosophy, physics, physiology, psychology, and ethics), but states there are similar concepts in other disciplines that he has not covered.[35]

Tao/dao means "a way" or "a road" as through one's field or to the village. It also describes the manner in which something can be done, such as making something.[36] It also means the "principle," "norm of conduct," "the rational principle in man," and "reason in man and reality."[37] It is that which orders one's inner life by balancing the conflicting forces. Liu further defines *tao* as:

> . . . the ordering one's inner life, the securing of proper balance between conflicting tendencies in one's nature, the relation that subsists between man and the natural world-order as well as between man and his fellows.[38]

---

32. Moore, *Chinese Mind*, 111.

33. Ball, *Essence of Tao*, 56.

34. Cunshan, "Differentiation of the Meaning of Qi," 194.

35. Ibid., 211.

36. Littlejohn, *Introduction to Daoism*, 1.

37. Liu, "Origin of Taoism," 376–77.

38. Ibid., 379.

Taoism describes the two primary forces that created the world through their action and reaction of yin-yang. It explains how organic and inorganic things work. The proper balance between the two leads to the way of life while extremes do not.[39]

> The principle of yin-yang is in fact an explanation of the behavior of organic and inorganic things in the universe as well as the invisible energy that infuses the cosmos . . . The concept incorporates the creation, interaction, and extinction of all things in an unending cycle.[40]

In Taoist thinking, everything in the world can be either *yin* or *yang*. Heaven is *yang* and earth is *yin*. Although the world is divided into yin and yang, they are not separate but one, as seen in the yin-yang symbol ☯.[41] Wang states, "They are also the rhythm and harmony of *qi*, the condensation and development, or the withdrawing into the depths or the surging to the exterior."[42]

Taoism divides the world into five elements: water, fire, wood, metal, earth, within which yin-yang forces work. The earth was considered neutral, while the other four elements correspond to the four directions and four seasons. They were also assigned colors and animals. See Table 1 below.

	Wood	Fire	Earth	Metal	Water
Season	Spring	Summer	Late Summer	Autumn	Winter
Direction	East	South	Center	West	North
Climate	Wind	Heat	Dampness	Dryness	Cold
Color	Blue/Green	Red	Yellow	White	Blue/Black
Animal	Dragon	Phoenix		Tiger	Tortoise/snake

Table 1: The Five Elements[43]

The interaction of yin-yang is not only as opposites; when the yin and yang have reached their peak they return to the other. This same principle is used to describe people's activities. Kohn explains that when a person has a goal

39. Ibid., 379.
40. De Mente, *Chinese Mind*, 19.
41. Ball, *Essence of Tao*, 111.
42. Wang, *Yinyang*, 81.
43. Ball, *Essence of Tao*, 129.

they should first draw back from that goal before going towards that goal. In that way their movement towards the goal becomes strengthened.[44]

Although Taoism's belief about human behavior is defined as *wu wei* (translated as "do nothing"), it means that things are done in a Taoist way rather than not doing anything.[45] This "non-action" is thought to enable the *tao* to flow freely and to allow the cosmic energy (*tao*) to flow through a person in order to achieve peace and harmony. The Taoist sets an example for others to do the same, thus creating an ideal community that is in tune with the universe.[46] By following the *tao* a person can change the situations that have been created by institutions, rules, and distinctions that lead to greed, suffering, and violence.[47] Following the *tao* also helps a person to not take sides in an argument but to help find the "middle way." Taoist thinking does not try to resolve contradictions, but uses contradiction to better understand the situation or to embrace both viewpoints. Taoist thinking also places greater importance on finding solutions to disagreements rather than proving one to be right and the other to be wrong. The goal is not fairness but to reduce the bad feelings between people.[48] The middle way is important because it fosters harmony in a society in which the focus is on the family and community. People are encouraged to be self-restraining for the good of the family/community.[49]

Cultivating the body is also a part of Taoism because the body consists of *qi*, the vital energy. Traditional Chinese medicine is based on yin-yang principles that enhance healing and health.[50] This includes not only eating certain foods at certain times but also enabling the *qi* to flow by removing blockages.

The Taoist belief of doing nothing is the opposite of Confucian social roles. However, this contradiction is also similar to Asian thinking—not completely one or the other. Contradictions and paradoxes arise from the interaction of the yin-yang principle like the positive and negative aspects that complement each other.[51]

---

44. Kohn, *Introducing Daoism*, 25.

45. Littlejohn, *Introduction to Daoism*, 19.

46. Kohn, *Introducing Daoism*, 27.

47. Littlejohn, *Introduction to Daoism*, 18–19.

48. Nesbitt, *Geography of Thought*, 27, 32, 75.

49. Ibid., 5–6.

50. Kohn, *Introducing Daoism*, 54–56.

51. Lin, "Chinese Mind," 260.

Reciprocity, Harmony, and Scripture

There are many aspects of Buddhist and Taoist thinking that are similar to passages in the Bible. In section 1 we saw how Asian cultures are similar to the culture of first-century Christians. Confucian beliefs reinforce the Strong Structure of the Hierarchical Asian culture (chapter 9) that develops respect for people, particularly in higher social positions. Buddhist and Taoist beliefs reinforce Strong Community through reciprocity and the desire for unity and harmony.

Reciprocity in Scripture

Caring for one another is a characteristic of Strong Community cultures and includes the sharing of resources, time, etc. similar to the Hebrew culture. The act of sharing is compared with sowing and reaping in the Scriptures. We receive what we give (Matt 5:7; Luke 6:38; Gal 6:7–10). If we sow more, we reap more or have a larger harvest (2 Cor 9:6). We are also to sow righteousness in order to reap love (Hos 10:12).

There are a number of passages that describe the reciprocity expected of relationships. Based on who we are as God's people, we are to show mercy and compassion to one another (Zech 7:9; Eph 4:32; 1 Pet 1:22), be devoted to and honor one another (Rom 12:10), be indebted to love for one another (Rom 13:8), serve one another (Gal 5:13), bear one another in love (Eph 4:2), submit to one another (Eph 5:21), build up and encourage one another to do good works (1 Thes 5:11; Heb 10:24; 13:13), and offer hospitality (Heb 4:9). We are also to stop passing judgment on others (Rom 14:13).

In chapter 3 Ben compared Asian grace to Global Grace, the kind of giving or reciprocating that is culturally shaped. The reason believers are to reciprocate to others is based on what Christ did for us. We are to love others just as Christ loved us (John 13:34), accept one another as Christ has accepted us (Rom 15:7), and forgive one another as Christ has forgiven us (Col 3:13). Buddhist reciprocity gives with the expectation that something will be given in return, but we are to share our resources because of what Christ has given us.

Unity in Scripture

Unity and harmony are also typical characteristics of Strong Community cultures. However, Asian unity is typically maintained by top-down decisions of authority figures. Lower-status people are expected to agree in order to have an outward appearance of harmony. This outward appearance is a false sense of harmony. However, the unity and harmony we are commanded to have is based on our relationship with God (John 17:23). With the help of the Holy Spirit we should be eager for unity (Eph 4:3). When there is unity among group members, it is good and pleasant (Ps 133:1). It is God's love that binds us together in unity (Col 3:14), with agreement and not divisions (1 Cor 1:10).

Section 3 presents examples of how Ben and Sheryl have untangled cultural complexities in their lives and ministry and discovered ways to experience God's grace more fully. The section concludes with suggestions for what the Asian American church might look like when the cultural complexities are untangled.

Reflection Questions

1. Briefly describe a recent conflict in your family or your ministry in which you were involved.

2. In what ways do you see reciprocity, false harmony, or face operating in this conflict?

3. Reflect on Ps 34:5; 105:4; 1 Cor 12:14—16:21; 2 Cor 4:6; and 1 Pet 2:6 for twenty minutes and write down what God is speaking to you about as a result of reflecting on these issues.

SECTION 3

Untangling Cultural Complexities and Weaving a Tapestry of Grace

IN SECTION 1 BEN described a number of issues in the Asian American church that arise from the cultural complexities between the first- and second-generation Asian American churches. In chapter 1 he showed how the silent exodus of the second and succeeding generations has formed different church models as the younger generations moved away from the immigrant church. In chapter 2 we saw how the Asian concepts of honor and shame influence a number of situations in Asian American life and ministry. Chapter 3 revealed the lack of understanding of biblical grace that arises from cultural influences, both Western and Asian. Chapter 4 explored the challenges of second-generation leaders who consider church planting, and chapter 5 showed how Asian culture shapes spiritual practices in the Asian American church.

In section 2 Sheryl presented a number of theological and cultural insights about the cultural complexities of the Asian American experience. In chapter 6 we saw the importance of defining ourselves as created in the image of God. Chapter 7 used a theory of culture to reveal the major difference between Asian and American cultures. In chapter 8 Sheryl explained how Asian and American cultures have a different definition of the person and how cultural values are maintained in language. Chapter 9 revealed how Confucian beliefs create a Strong Structure culture with strong cultural expectations for behavior, and chapter 10 showed how Buddhist reciprocity and Taoist harmony create Strong Community. These three Asian belief systems are the opposite of the cultural values of typical American culture.

We also saw that many Asian cultural practices are similar to Scripture except that the underlying motivation may not be "as unto the Lord."

In section 3 Ben (chapter 11) and Sheryl (chapter 12) share their own personal journeys of cultural self-discovery and how much Asian thinking shaped their lives in spite of not being first-generation Asian Americans. They share how their cultural beliefs prevented them from understanding God's grace, and how God moved in their lives to enable them to experience his grace more fully. Ben concludes (chapter 13) with suggestions for how understanding Asian and American culture can help Asian Americans untangle the cultural complexities that prevent them from experiencing God's grace more fully.

11

Ben's Journey to Grace

As a child growing up in Pasadena, California, an only child to my parents in the 1960s and seventies, the television became the extra friend or family member that I never had. Watching shows and living vicariously through episodes of *The Monkees* hoping to become a musician and *The Brady Bunch* wanting to have multiple siblings was a weekly ritual. This was exacerbated by the fact that being an only Asian American child can be very lonesome. There was also the overprotectiveness by my parents and the fact that I was the only Asian American in my school in Pasadena, California, during the 1960s. My childhood experiences left me unaware of being Asian American. This lack of awareness of being Asian was due, in large part, to the fact that I was surrounded by Caucasians, both in school and in church. I basically thought that I, too, was "white," and that the only difference was the color of my skin. I was ignorant of my parents' early immigration history of coming to the United States in the 1950s, much before the big wave of immigration of Asians that began in 1963. I felt like I fit into my community in school and in church. But all this changed when I went away to college at the University of California, Los Angeles.

My Journey of Becoming Asian

Growing up in Pasadena during the 1960s and 1970s, everyone I knew was basically blond with blue eyes. Over the years, I met a few Asians like myself but, for the most part, we all just tried to fit in. It wasn't until I went away to college that my true identity as an Asian American began to emerge. After I missed the deadline to live in the dorms at UCLA, a friend recommended that I look into joining a Christian fraternity called Alpha Gamma Omega. I knew someone in the fraternity who went to my large Caucasian church, so I decided to join. I discovered two things while I was in the fraternity: 1) strong committed followers of Jesus and 2) Asian Americans who were more Asian than American. Both types of people were fascinating to me to watch and to learn from. I began to grow in my faith by leaps and bounds due to the strong teaching, the discipleship training, and the accountability of the brotherhood. But a second surprising realization began to take root: I began identifying more and more with my Asian identity. To explain simply, there were many Koreans, Chinese, and Japanese living in the fraternity. While the actual motto of the fraternity was—"the Christ-Centered fraternity," the second (and satirical) motto was—"the rice-centered fraternity" due to the many Asian members.

Talking with these Asian brothers, sharing Asian meals together, and being exposed to the various Asian cultures began a new journey in my life. It was there in college that I first began to embrace my Asian American identity. This was further reinforced through being a part of a new campus parachurch ministry called Korean American Christian Fellowship (KACF): a unique English-speaking Korean American ministry. During this time at UCLA, the other Korean Bible study was conducted in Korean. I did not speak Korean because I was raised in Pasadena and had rebelled against my culture, including learning Korean. But at KACF, for the first time, I felt right at home with other Asians who looked very Asian, but who spoke English like myself.

Calling Towards Ministry

It was during this time in college that I received my calling into pastoral ministry. Largely influenced by the KACF Bible study and my time under the teaching of Pastor John MacArthur from Grace Community Church, I knew that God wanted me to preach and minister to people as my calling in life. This calling would be challenged by my parents, who wanted me to go to law school instead of seminary. They were adamantly against my decision to go into ministry. Obviously, from an Asian perspective being a lawyer would be more prestigious and financially rewarding than being a pastor. And since I was an only child, a male for that matter, I was torn. So now I was faced with a dilemma: obey my parents or follow my calling to the ministry. As it turns out I could do both, but only through a lengthy process. I got a full-time job working forty hours a week while also serving as a Sunday School teacher at the church. I did this faithfully for three years.

I learned so much during this time. I learned the value of hard work, of saving money, of going through the daily grind of traffic, and of learning to be a witness for Christ in the marketplace. While I did this, God was working both in my heart and also in my parents' hearts.

As a result, two incredibly priceless lessons arose from this. First, my calling to the ministry increased and was confirmed in a greater way because I was not serving full-time in the ministry. I had no greater desire than to go into the ministry. If making money in the workplace became my passion, then I would know that the calling towards ministry was not what God had for me. But the exact opposite occurred. This was wonderfully assuring to me. Second, a greater lesson learned was that my parents saw my diligence and commitment and eventually blessed me to go to seminary to pursue full-time ministry as a career. The lesson here was that present obedience led to future opportunity. I could easily have disobeyed my parents' wish to forgo seminary, but I later realized that would not have yielded the same result had I not honored them. From my parents' perspective, they were unsure if I could do a good job of being a pastor since they had only seen me in limited situations where I proved to be more irresponsible than trustworthy. Once they saw that I was actually diligent and responsible as a person, they felt more assured in allowing me to be a pastor. According to my parents, they weren't sure if I could take care of other people since I hadn't proven that I could take care of myself. Once I proved myself, they began to affirm me.

My Training in Seminary and in the Korean Church

My first experience came as a youth pastor in a Korean church in a small secluded city in the San Gabriel Valley called El Monte. My interview for the job was both memorable and hilarious. I was asked to come and meet the elders of the church for the position. I brought a letter of recommendation from Pastor John MacArthur, the famed Bible pastor/teacher from Grace Community Church. I dressed up in a three-piece suit when I went to the church for the interview. To my surprise, the elders were dressed in shorts and t-shirts. When I handed them the recommendation, it turned out that they did not know who John MacArthur was, so the recommendation made no difference at all. They asked me only one question in the interview. The question was, "How soon can you start?" I was on the fast track. I started serving at the church the next day. I worked all Saturday night to prepare my first message. I served in this church for the next fifteen years. This was the first church I pastored.

One of the biggest struggles I had during my time as a pastor in this Korean church was that I did not speak the Korean language nor was I familiar with the culture. These were huge disadvantages for me. I unknowingly offended many people because I was raised in a non-Asian environment and was not aware of the differences in social etiquette. For example, I did not realize that the questions I was asked by the elders were actually imperatives rather than suggestions. Also, I often misunderstood the nature of the indirect communication from the church leaders and sometimes I even ignored indirect messages. I basically broke every cultural boundary and rule there was. My actions certainly got me in trouble, but the church was gracious to have me, an ignorant, Westernized Asian American, serve as their pastor for so long.

Conclusion

When people ask me, "How long did it take to write this book?" My answer is: "Twenty-five years—twenty-four years to learn the lessons and one year to actually write down the lessons." I often tell people that my life journey has been a process of learning to become an Asian American. You see, I've spent twenty-five years in the Caucasian church and now twenty-seven years in Asian churches. While not all of my experiences have necessarily been good ones, they have for the most part been valuable ones. The experiences and circumstances that I faced in both church contexts have significantly helped and shaped me in understanding how culture impacts the church. Whether it be the Western culture of a Caucasian Congregational church or the Asian culture of the Korean Presbyterian church, both perspectives certainly have good and bad aspects to them. While there is no perfect culture, because of the Fall, there are also many redeemable and valuable parts of every culture as well.

Currently, my family attends a Korean American church in Los Angeles. I'm not a pastor anymore, but I still have many opportunities to preach at churches fairly often. My role now is to encourage, support, and be a friend to Asian American pastors. Through my role at Talbot School of Theology, I have the opportunity to serve as a safe, neutral person who can listen, counsel, and encourage pastors and leaders from many Asian American churches from across the nation. In addition, Talbot has provided support for the master's level class "The Asian Church in American Society," which I teach with Dr. Sheryl Takagi Silzer. The seminary also supports the Asian American Doctor of Ministry cohort we teach each summer.

The future of the Asian American church looks very promising. While many mainline churches and denominations are in decline, the Asian American church and parachurch ministries continue to grow. I'm thankful for opportunities to continue learning and teaching on the subjects found in this book. As I grow, I continue to mature more and more in my journey of becoming an Asian American in my own story and identity. My concluding thanksgiving comes from Paul's opening statement in Ephesians, "to the praise of his glorious grace, with which he has blessed us in the Beloved" (Eph 1:6).

12

Sheryl's Journey to Grace[1]

I (SHERYL) HAVE LIVED through three diagnoses of cancer, each associated with feelings of bitterness towards authority figures. The first diagnosis was breast cancer in 1993 shortly after my husband and I returned from living and working overseas as mission workers. During the previous two years living overseas I struggled with not having a role or place in the organization I worked for. My supervisor explained that I couldn't have an official role because my husband was the only one who had a work visa. I looked around for something to do to justify receiving support. I was interested in doing a graduate study program that would enable me to study the particular stresses of missionary women. My supervisor, however, did not approve of the topic because he felt women's struggles were his responsibility as our group leader. As a typical Asian, I was unable to voice my disagreement and I suppressed my negative feelings, allowing bitterness to develop.

The second diagnosis of cancer (uterine) I faced was in 2001 after I finished a PhD in Intercultural Studies from Fuller School of World Mission. Although the mission supervisor I had at that time had reluctantly given me permission to do the study program, he did not have a position for me to fill when I finished. Once again I could not voice my disagreement and I suppressed my negative feelings, allowing bitterness to continue.

The third diagnosis of cancer (esophageal) I received was in 2015 after I was given a job to do but the Asian American man who asked me to do it did not agree with what I did. At first I didn't understand what was happening, but later Ben helped me to realize that the man's reaction was the typical Asian way of saying he did not agree. Rather than confronting the Asian man and causing him to lose face, I realized I should find ways to make the work more acceptable. Rather than allowing the typical bitter

1. For more information about this subject, see Silzer, "Confessions," 5-12.

feelings to arise, I realized that God wanted me to respond differently than I had before.

As I spent some time reflecting on my relationship with my father, I realized that I had learned not to openly disagree with him or other authority figures. Instead I suppressed my negative feelings and this enabled bitterness to grow. Koreans have a word for this bitterness (*han*). Park defines *han* by saying, "*Han* can be defined by the critical wound of the heart generated by unjust psychosomatic repression, as well as by social, political, economic, and cultural oppression."[2]

I first became aware of Confucian values when I started researching Asian culture in preparation to teach the class at Talbot for Asian Americans preparing for or already in ministry in ethnic churches and parachurch ministries. As I prepared lectures on the influence of different religious beliefs of Asian cultures—Confucianism, Buddhism, and Taoism—I started to notice how tenets from these religions were not only similar to those in Christianity, but were also reflected in my own beliefs and behavior. At the same time I was also taking a course on spiritual formation, and one of the class assignments was to spend extended time in reflective prayer. It was during one of these times of reflection that I began to see how my upbringing in a Japanese American family had Confucian roots that did not reflect biblical values.

Although neither my parents nor my grandparents instructed me to follow Confucian customs, many of our family practices were Confucian. I have come to realize that the similarities between some Confucian practices and Christian practices made it easy for my family and other Asians to adopt Christianity. The similarities also led me to interpret my Asian cultural values as being biblical.

After a while I began to understand the Confucian values that influenced my family. My father was the oldest and only son, so he had the responsibility for his parents (filial piety) unlike my Caucasian friends. For many years my paternal grandparents lived in the same house as we did and then they moved to a small house next door. We often did things together, such as sharing meals and working on our small farm.

My parents normally responded to authority figures with complete obedience without question (subject to ruler) as taught in Confucian practice. When they and our other Japanese American relatives were placed in an internment camp during World War II, they never complained against

2. Park, *Wounded Heart of God*, 10.

the U.S. government. They did what the authority figures told them to do. They did not consider it appropriate to question authorities. So they, along with the rest of the Japanese living on the West coast, went to live in one of the ten internment camps for several years during the war.

In my adult life I found that I frequently disagreed with authority figures but could never bring myself to discuss my disagreement with them (following the subject to ruler obedience). Instead, I would suppress my negative feelings just as my parents had when they disagreed with authority figures. From my parents' example I concluded that disagreeing with authority figures was unbiblical (Rom 13:1).

My mother and my grandmother always submitted to my father and my grandfather (wife to husband). I never heard either of them contradict or question their husbands. If my mother ever disagreed with my father, I never saw it. In a similar way as an adult I complained to other people about my dissatisfaction with authority figures, but I could never bring myself to confront leaders face to face. I also had difficulty expressing my disagreement with my husband (wife to husband). When I was really upset, I would become quiet and distance myself from him rather than confront him. I thought this was the biblical way of handling conflict. I also didn't know how to address the bitterness that was building up inside of me as a result of my cultural preferences.

I had three brothers (an older brother by one and half years and two younger brothers seven and eleven years younger) and no sisters. When we were growing up, my older brother and I were expected to take responsibility for our younger brothers (older to younger). We had to look after them and watch them while my parents worked.

The Confucian value of fidelity of friends was not as evident in my childhood because all my family's friends were Caucasian. Although my parents had a number of good friends when we were growing up, they seemed to drift away later in life. Maybe this was the influence of the American culture. After my father passed away my mother complained to me about her Caucasian friends. At first I thought she was as American as I was until she explained the situations. My mother's friends needed various kinds of help which my mother didn't mind doing (such as driving them from place to place or helping them shop because their eyes were not as good), but she was disappointed because they often did not reciprocate in any way. If they had offered to give money for gas or had given her something to reciprocate her for her help, she would have felt better. She couldn't tell them her feelings directly. She found ways of saying no to their requests without actually saying "no" (friend to friend).

The role of women in Confucian thought is to submit to men. This pattern was very evident in my life. Even though my mother never complained about having to move in with her in-laws when she married my father, she later insisted that she would never put any of her children through the same situation. As the only daughter in my family I often thought it wasn't fair that I had to do more work than my older brother and did not have the same privileges. However, I could never complain openly to my parents. I felt it was what God expected me to do. My oldest brother took responsibility for my mother when my father passed away and my mother looked to him for major decision-making. As the only daughter with three brothers, and later, as a married woman with two sons and no daughters, I felt the duty of a woman was to take care of the men in my life before I took care of myself.

Shortly after college, I felt God's call to join a mission organization (Wycliffe Bible Translators). During my forty plus years with the organization, I have had difficulty with various supervisors. God began to help me see that my difficulty with supervisors came from Asian cultural influences my parents passed on to me. The difficulty I had in confronting authority figures came from believing that it was not biblical to disagree with an authority figure. I couldn't understand why I felt so bad if submitting to authorities was my biblical duty.

Additionally, because I believed men should be treated better than women, I viewed myself as less valuable in God's eyes. This belief was evident in how I treated myself. I would put men above me or give them preferential treatment, but I did not like it. This also contributed to my bitterness. I tried to get rid of the bitterness by working harder and doing more things, particularly in ministry. I thought I just needed to do more things in order for God to be pleased with me. If others praised me for the things I did, then God would also be pleased. If I didn't get noticed or praised for the things I did, I thought God wasn't pleased with me. My mistaken belief just made me work harder and led to more stress and more bitterness.

As I studied Scripture, I saw differences between Christian motivations and the motivation behind some of my Asian cultural values. Christians are to relate to others based our identity in Christ and who he is. I submitted to authority figures, but I was not doing it the way Christ wanted me to do it—out of reverence for God. Therefore, bitterness built up inside of me.

When God began to help me with getting rid of this bitterness, a heavy burden seemed to lift. I began to see authority figures from God's perspective and became less judgmental. I still have a long way to go as I have years of bitter feelings built up inside of me, including the feelings passed down to me through my grandmother and my mother. I didn't realize how much I was starving for God's grace in my life and how my bitterness prevented me from experiencing God's grace.

Fulfilling the social roles of the Confucian hierarchy by submitting to elders is the ideal for Asians. Following social norms can easily be interpreted as following biblical commands to submit to authority figures (Rom 13:1). The Bible also teaches that by not submitting to authority figures we rebel against God's command and invite judgment (Rom 13:2). By following Confucian logic we might think that our actions also add to God's desire to accept us. Confucian reciprocity may lead us to believe that God will save us if we follow his commands. However, it is by God's grace that we are saved and not by our works (e.g., being submissive to authority figures) (Eph 2:8–9). Christ died once for all for our sins to bring us to God (1 Pet 3:18). Discovering my Confucian, Buddhist, and Taoist roots and comparing my resulting responses to others with Scripture was the first step towards enabling God's grace in my life.

Reflection Questions

1. In what ways do you identify with either Ben's or Sheryl's story?

2. How did the underlying Asian cultural values result in cultural clashes?

3. What are the cultural values you want to replace with biblical beliefs in order to experience God's grace more fully?

13

Mapping Out the Future of the Asian American Church

So where does the Asian American church go from here? We've seen how the Asian American church continues to face challenges between the first and second generations in a number of areas including the silent exodus of the younger generation. Our desire is to not only reverse this trend, but to also see God's grace flowing freely within Asian American churches. A tapestry of grace includes greater cultural self-awareness of all generations, the ability to discern cultural beliefs from biblical truths, and a greater reliance on God's help for resolving existing misunderstandings and conflicts.

But to begin with, we need to go back to the basics and examine whether we are able to accept ourselves as God created us—in his image. If we are able to accept this truth, this truth will be evident in our relationships with others. We will be able to respond to others (older or younger) as also created in God's image. We can also enhance our understanding that this truth is culturally influenced—Americans interpret individuals as created in God's image; Asians interpret the group as created in God's image. After we have recognized and accepted how we were made, then we can examine whether our responses to the other culture are a result of our cultural beliefs, and whether we, as well as they, are experiencing God's grace. If not, there might still be some cultural complexities we have not untangled. We need to continually ask God for his wisdom to untangle the cultural complexities in order for God's grace to flow through us. We have done our best to give some insights and instruction about how culture plays a significant part in the Asian American churches. What opportunities lie ahead for the Asian American church? What actions can we take to untangle the cultural complexities so as to weave a tapestry of God's grace?

Three Opportunities for the Future

Now that we have a clearer understanding of the cultural complexities we face, there are three opportunities we can use to build towards the future of the Asian American church: 1) specialized ministries in the church, 2) better leadership strategies and standards, and 3) more grace-based preaching and teaching.

Specialized Ministries in the Church

The nature of specialized ministries in the church is to target situations and circumstances that may initially seem shameful and embarrassing for Asian Americans to discuss. This would include the whole gamut of counseling, especially for people struggling with addictions, divorce, and the need for marriage counseling. Counseling is still stigmatized within the Asian community due to the high level of shame in the culture. Fortunately, this shame culture seems to be decreasing as the generations get younger and younger. Asian American churches are even beginning to hire professional counselors and counseling pastors to work in the church in order to provide counseling for church members. This kind of ministry would have been unheard of even a decade ago. But with the hardships of society and the greater needs of the community, it is extremely wise and beneficial to have counselors available within and through the church. Grief counseling can be yet another type of ministry that churches can make available for helping families dealing with the loss of a loved one through suicide or for helping unwed young girls who are overcoming trauma from abortions. These kinds of situations are extremely shameful for families and for the longest time have largely been ignored within the Asian American church.

Specialized ministries can also serve church members in a positive way through instruction and preparation for the future. Training for young couples and parents to help them with rearing their children are much needed for today's Asian American church. Past generations did not have this type of ministry nor did they see the need for it. But now, as many families are dual-income parents, the lack of time and knowledge for raising children are at an all-time high. For this reason, the Asian American church should come alongside these parents to instruct and encourage them as well as to provide support during this new and challenging time.

Better Leadership Standards and Strategies

Another very important opportunity for the future comes in the form of better leadership strategies and standards for the church. Since many Asian American churches have not been in existence for more than a generation, the procedures and practices related to leadership are relatively new and not well developed. This will certainly improve as time goes on. While many Westernized megachurches have strong systems and procedures in place for nearly every situation, the Asian American church is still discovering and identifying the unique challenges and struggles of being Asian American. Again, this is where the cultural aspects of ministry in an Asian context are very different from mainstream American culture. The contrast between the needs of non-Asian American churches and Asian American churches is very noticeable in the seminary training that occurs throughout America. The principles of leadership taught at most seminaries and the books that are written about church leadership are all geared towards American models of leadership. Many of these principles do not work in an Asian context. For example, the Asian culture is typically hierarchical in terms of leadership based on age, gender, and status. This in turn requires honorific references to the leader rather than an informal or casual use of first names. In addition, the requirement of submission to leaders, again largely due to the Confucian influence, would not even be questioned in an Asian context. But in an American church context, all of these examples would be quite different. In the American context perspectives of leadership are much more egalitarian. Informal titles addressing leadership, being on a first-name basis, and even developing friendships with leaders are common practices. Submission is not the first response Americans have, and discussion and even disagreement is allowable. Asian leaders would tend to be more concerned about the family as a whole rather than just the individual and care for people would most likely integrate spiritual and material issues, while they would be separated in an Americanized or Western church. These are but a few of the many differences in leadership standards between the two cultures.

Selection of leadership poses yet another different scenario. Qualities of character and competency for leadership are highly valued in the West. A person's unique gifting and fit are closely scrutinized in order to find an appropriate leader. In the Asian contexts, however, relationships and reciprocity for leadership selection have been the standards. This leads back to the idea of Global Grace (GG) that has traces of first-century practices of patronage. Part of the issue here for the second generation is that they have not seen clear procedures and protocols for leadership selection. For this reason, they only mimic what they have seen in the past. Adding to this, they were not privileged to know why certain leaders were selected, leaving the process of selection open to much speculation. As a result, many second-generation leaders simply do not know how to select leaders. The default choice then becomes those members who have been around the longest or those who may be the oldest. Neither of these principles is not necessarily a good or a biblical way to select leaders.

The biggest struggle for leadership strategy in the Asian American church has been the poor execution of leadership succession. In many cases, since there are no clear examples of this, the lack of experience in this process is evident. The Asian American church needs to start setting up proper procedures for selecting leaders, including qualifications, voting processes, time frames for the process, and specific job descriptions that will aid in selecting the best leaders. In addition to this process, the leader who is stepping down needs to be sure to not only pass on the responsibility to the incoming leader but also to give the leader all of the needed authority as well. Without a clear procedure, the transition process will become messy and will not be complete. Leadership succession, in this author's opinion, is probably the most challenging obstacle for the next generation of Asian American leaders. There simply are not many good examples for people to follow. Leaders in the Asian American church need to find ways to plan well for the future and to insure a smooth transition for all.

More Grace-based Teaching and Preaching

Since Asian Americans are primarily duty-bound, the message of grace given through teaching and preaching, as well as through the example of the leaders will provide great encouragement and relief to the members of the church. As mentioned earlier, this is one of the reasons that the Gospel-centered preaching style is so appealing to second-generation Asian Americans. Grace as a motivation will always prove to be stronger, better, and longer lasting for any believer, but especially for Asian American Christians. Again, because grace is typically not shown in Asian churches, many second and succeeding generations of Asian Americans flock to the different Hotel models of churches that are primarily multiethnic and grace-oriented. Grace, then, can replace duty and the emphasis on good works that are both explicitly and implicitly conveyed within the Asian American church.

In addition to the teaching, grace needs to be modeled in such a way that the leadership exudes this important Christian value. This speaks to the leadership style of the pastor. A pastor's style should not be an autocratic and hierarchical style of leadership, but rather one of servant-leadership that demonstrates Christlikeness. Demanding, manipulating, commanding, and forcing members to follow the leader has no place in the Christian church (Mark 10:42). Rather, the leadership should model grace and truth just as Christ did.

Shaping the Future for a Better Asian American Church

Practically then, what is needed to shape the future of the Asian American church? I want to suggest three points: 1) learning from mentors; 2) contextualizing like missionaries; and 3) be discerning of the Scriptures like the Bereans in Acts 17:11. These practices will prove to be safeguards that should insure a better, more stable future for the Asian American church.

Learning from Seasoned Mentors

Mentorship is such an important part of learning and growing. Paul served as a mentor to Timothy (2 Tim 2:2). Older men and women are to mentor and train up younger men and women (Titus 2:2-8). And younger churches (i.e., Asian American churches) can learn from and be mentored by older churches (i.e., the immigrant church). The transfer of wisdom is essential for growth and development. Proverbs 3:13 tells us, "Blessed is the one who finds wisdom, and the one who gets understanding." Proverbs 19:20 tells us, "Listen to advice and accept instruction, that you may gain wisdom in the future." The second-generation Asian American church may not agree with everything that the first-generation church does, but it would be foolish to not listen to anything that they pass on. There can be "nuggets" of truth that come from the immigrant church, even if the wisdom may be regarding mistakes that have been made in the past. The younger generation should be quick to listen and learn rather than be dismissive of possible valuable lessons (Jas 1:19). Hearing the stories and learning the history of older saints, individuals, and churches from the past are priceless activities because they demonstrate important lessons to be learned for the future.

Contextualizing Like Missionaries

One of the best approaches to ministry in the Asian American church is to think and act like a missionary. Any effective missionary understands the need to contextualize the Gospel message to the culture in order to have influence and impact with the people. First Corinthians 9:19–23 is the best example of this kind of contextualization. In this passage, the Apostle Paul writes that he became like others (e.g., a Jew, one under the law, a weak person, etc.) in order that he might win them for Christ. Paul never compromised his values. At the same time, he understood the importance of identifying with his audience to understand them and ultimately to minister to them so that they would know Christ. Second-generation Asian Americans can benefit greatly by taking this same approach in order to understand the differences between Asian and American cultures to be able to build relationships with the first-generation church despite these differences. This will prove to be the best mission work possible if second-generation Asian Americans can effectively reach first-generation Asians and vice versa within their own churches.

Be Discerning of the Scriptures Like the Bereans

In Acts 17:11, we are told that the Bereans scrutinized the teaching of the Apostle Paul. The passage tells us that "they received the word with all eagerness, examining the Scriptures daily to see if these things were so." In order for all of us to build a better and stronger Asian American church for the future, we need to follow the blueprints of the Scripture, the Word of God. Without knowing the timeless principles of God's Word, we would be lost and would only develop another secular organization. Knowing the Word of God well begins with the leadership of the church, and then needs to continue with the older members of the church. The education department of the church needs to teach the Bible and not just moralism. Through the content of the Word of God, along with the leading of the Spirit of God, greater works for the church can be accomplished. But this will require a commitment by the whole generation of Asian Americans for now and forevermore.

Final Challenge

Our desire for this book has been to help current and future Asian Americans to not only build stronger, healthier, and growing churches to reach the many unchurched Asian Americans throughout the U.S., but also to reverse/address the silent exodus from the immigrant church The Asian American church population has been growing over the last decade, and we pray that these churches would glorify and honor the Lord Jesus Christ through their efforts. We also pray that this book has provided some guidance and direction towards this goal. May God receive all the glory! Amen!

Bibliography

Ademek, Wendi L. "The Impossibility of the Given: Representations of Merit and Emptiness in Medieval Chinese Buddhism." *History of Religions* 45 (2005) 133–80.

Althen, Gary. *American Way: A Cultural Guide to the United States.* Boston, MA: Nicholas Brealey, 2011.

The Analects I:11, XII:2, XIII:18, XV:23.

Atkins, Richard A. Jr. *Egalitarian Community: Ethnography and Exegesis.* Tuscaloosa, AL: University of Alabama Press, 1991.

Austin, Lewis, ed. *Japan: the Paradox of Progress.* New Haven: Yale University Press, 1976.

Ball, Pamela. *The Essence of Tao.* Herrfortshire, UK: Eagle Editions, 2004.

Barclay, John. *Paul and the Gift.* Grand Rapids, MI: Eerdmans, 2015.

Bean, Andrea. "In Light of Anatman: Toward a Feminist No-self." *Journal of Theta Alpha Kappa* 34 (2010) 18–31.

Bellah, Robert N., et al. *Habits of the Heart: Individualism and Commitment in American Life.* London, UK: University of California Press, 1985.

Benedict, Ruth. *The Sword and The Chrysanthemum: Patterns of Japanese Culture.* Boston, MA: Houghton Mifflin, 1946.

Bhagat, M. G. *Ancient Indian Asceticism.* New Delhi: Munshiram Manoharlal, 1976.

The Book of Filial Piety. http://www.chinapage.com/confucius/xiaojing-be.html.

The Book of Rites, 2:1.

Brown, Brene. *Daring Greatly.* New York, NY: Gotham, 2012.

Brown, Lucien. "Contrasts Between Korean and Japanese Honorifics." *Sapienza-Univerisita di Roma,* 82 (2008) 369–85.

Byon, Andrew Sangpil. "Teaching Refusals in Korean." *Korean Language in America* 10 (2005) 1–19.

Cardon, P. W., and J. C. Scott. "Chinese Business Face: Communication Behaviors and Teaching Approaches." *Business Communication Quarterly* 66 (2003) 9–22.

Cha, Peter, and Grace May. "Gender Relations in Healthy Households." In *Growing Healthy Asian American Churches: Ministry Insights from Groundbreaking Congregations,* edited by Peter Cha et al., 164–82. Downers Grove, IL: InterVarsity, 2006.

Cha, Peter, et al. "Multigenerational Households." In *Growing Healthy Asian American Churches: Ministry Insights from Groundbreaking Congregations,* edited by Peter Cha et al., 145–63. Downers Grove, IL: InterVarsity, 2006.

Chafer, Lewis Sperry. *Grace: The Glorious Theme.* Grand Rapids: Zondervan, 1950.

Chang, Hui-Ching. "Harmony as Performance: The Turbulence under Chinese Interpersonal Communication." *Discourse Studies* 3 (May 2001) 155–79.

Cheng, Chung-Ying. *New Dimensions of Confucian and Neo-Confucian Philosophy.* Albany, NY: SUNY Press, 1991.

Cho, Young-mee Yu, and Peter Sells. "A Lexical Account of Inflectional Suffixes in Korean." *Journal of East Asian Linguistics* 4 (1995) 119–74.

Choo, Miho. "Teaching Language Styles of Korean." *The Korean Language in America* 3 (1999) 77–95.

Choong, Gary K. G. *Counter-Cultural Paradigmatic Leadership: Ethic Use of Power in Confucian Societies.* Eugene, OR: Wipf and Stock, 2011.

Coleman, Samuel. "Teaching Culture in the Japanese Language Programs: Insights from the Social and Behavioral Sciences." *Japanese Language and Literature* 43 (2008) 319–33.

Cunshan, Li. "A Differentiation of the Meaning of Qi on Several Different Levels." *Frontiers of Philosophy in China* 3 (2008) 194–212.

Daniels, Peter T., and William Bright. *The World's Writing Systems.* Oxford, NY: Oxford University Press, 1996.

De Mente, Boye Lafayette. *The Chinese Mind: Understanding Traditional Chinese Beliefs and Their Influence on Contemporary Culture.* Clarendon, VT: Tuttle, 2009.

DeSilva, David. *Despising Shame: Honor Discourse and Community Maintenance in the Epistle to the Hebrews.* Atlanta, GA: Society of Biblical Literature, 1996.

———. *Honor, Patronage, Kinship and Purity: Unlocking New Testament Culture.* Downers Grove, IL: InterVarsity Academic, 2000.

Dickson, Kazuo Yagi. "Protestant Perspectives on Ancestor Worship in Japanese Buddhism: The Funeral and the Buddhist Altar." *Buddhist-Christian Studies* 15 (1995) 43–59.

Douglas, Mary T. "Cultural Bias." In *In the Active Voice.* 1st ed., 183–254. London, UK: Routledge, Kegan and Paul, 1982.

———. *How Institutions Think.* NY: Syracuse University Press, 1987.

———. *Risk and Blame: Essays in Cultural Theory.* London: Routledge, 1992.

"Elderly Protection Law." China. http://www.npc.gov.cn/npc/xinwen/lfgz/flca/2012–07/06/content_1729109.htm.

Elliott, Matthew. *Faithful Feelings: Rethinking Emotions in the New Testament.* Grand Rapids, MI: Kregel, 2006.

Erickson, Millard. *Christian Theology.* Grand Rapids, MI: Baker, 1992.

Fairbank, John K. *The United States and China.* Rev. ed. New York: Viking, 1958.

Flanders, Christopher. *About Face: Rethinking Face for the 21st Century.* Eugene, OR: Pickwick Publication. American Society of Missiology Monograph Series 9, 2011.

———. "Fixing the Problem of Face." *Evangelical Missions Quarterly* 45 (Jan 2009) 12–19.

Friedman, Ray, et al. "An Expectancy Model of Chinese American Differences in Conflict Avoiding." *Journal of International Business Studies* 37 (2006) 76–91.

Gee, Tracy. "From Swallowing Suffering." In *More than Serving Tea: Asian American Women on Expectations, Relationships, Leadership and Faith,* edited by Nikki A. Toyama and Tracey Gee, 69–85. Downers Grove, IL: InterVarsity, 2006.

Georg, Stefan, et al. "Telling General Linguists about Altaic." *Journal of Linguistics* 35 (1999) 65–98.

Goffman, Erving. "On Facework: An Analysis of Ritual Elements in Social Interaction." *Psychiatry,* 18 (1955) 213–231.

Grayson, James Huntley. "The Kwallye Samga of Korea: A Failed Attempt at Christian Accommodation to Confucian Culture." *Asian Folklore Studies* 66 (2007) 125–40.

Hals, Ronald M. *Grace and Faith in the Old Testament.* Minneapolis, MN: Augsburg, 1980.

Haugh, Michael, and Carl Hinze. "A Metalinguistic Approach to Deconstructing the Concepts of 'Face' and 'Politeness' in Chinese, English and Japanese." *Journal of Pragmatics* 35 (2003) 1581–1611.

Hellerman, Joseph H. *Embracing Shared Ministry: Power and Status in the Early Church and Why It Matters Today.* Grand Rapids. MI: Kregel, 2013.

———. *Reconstructing Honor in Roman Philippi: Carmen Christi as Cursus Pudorum.* Society for New Testament Studies Monograph Series. Cambridge: Cambridge University Press, 2008.

Herr, Ranjoo Seodu. "Is Confucianism Compatible with Care Ethics?" *Philosophy East and West* 53 (2003) 471–89.

Hitchcock, David L. *Asian Values and the United States: How Much Conflict?* (Washington, D.C.: Center for Strategic and International Studies, 1994.

Ho, David Yau-Fai. "Filial Piety, Authoritarian Moralism, and Cognitive Conservatism in Chinese Societies." *Genetic, Social and General Psychology Monograph* 120 (August 1994) 349–65.

———. "On the Concept of Face." *American Journal of Sociology* 81 (1976) 867–84.

———. "Relational Orientation and Methodological Relationalism." *Bulletin of the Hong Kong Psychological Society* 26–27 (1991) 81–95.

Hoekema, Andrew. *Created in God's Image.* Grand Rapids, MI: Eerdmans, 1994.

Hofstede, Geerdt. *Culture's Consequences: Comparing Values, Behaviors, Institutions and Organizations Across Cultures.* 2nd ed. Thousand Oaks, CA: Sage, 2001.

———. "Individualism, China." http://geert-hofstede.com/china.html.

———. "Individualism, Japan." http://geert-hofstede.com/japan.html.

———. "Individualism, South Korea." http://geert-hofstede.com/south-korea.html.

———. "Individualism, United States." http://geert-hofstede.com/united-states.html.

Hofstede, Geerdt, and Michael Minkor. "Long- versus Short-term Orientation: New Perspectives." *Asia Pacific Business Review* 16 (Oct 2010) 493–504.

Hong, Beverly. "Politeness in Chinese: Impersonal Pronouns and Personal Greetings." *Anthropological Linguistics* 27 (1985) 204–13.

Hsieh, Yu-Wei. "Filial Piety and Chinese Society." In *The Chinese Mind: Essentials of Chinese Philosophy and Culture*, edited by Charles A. Moore, 167–87. Honolulu, HI: University of Hawaii Press, 1968.

Hsu, Francis L. K. "Confucianism in Comparative Context." In *Confucianism and the Family,* edited by Walter H. Slote and George A. DeVos, 53–74. Albany, NY: SUNY Press, 1998.

Hu, Hsien Chin. "The Chinese Concepts of Face." *American Anthropologist* 46 (1944) 45–64.

Humphreys, Christmas. *Karma and Rebirth.* England, Surrey: Curzon, 1994.

Hwang, Kwang-Kuo. "Chinese Relationalism: Theoretical Constructions and Methodological Considerations." *Journal for the Theory of Social Behavior* 30 (2000) 155–78.

———. "Face and Favor: The Chinese Power Game." *American Journal of Sociology* 92 (1987) 944–74.

Hwang, Shin Ja Joo. *Discourse Features of Korean Narration.* Dallas, TX: The Summer Institute of Linguistics, 1987.

The I-Ching: The Book of Changes: The Great Appendix, Appendix 6. Translated by James Legge. Whitefish, MT: Kessinger Publications, 2012. http://baharna.com/iching/legge/Appendix%206%20%20Sequence%20of%20the%20Hexagrams.htm.

Ito, Youichi. "Socio-Cultural Backgrounds of Japanese Interpersonal Communication Style." *Les Enjeux du Futur* 39 (1989) 101–28.

Jeung, Russell. *Faithful Generations: Race and New Asian American Churches.* New Brunswick, NJ: Rutgers University Press, 2005.

Johnson, S. Lewis Jr. "God Gave Them up. A Study in Divine Retribution." *Biblioteca Sacra MSJ 21* (2010) 21–29.

Kang, Steve. "Conclusion: Measuring the Health of our Households." In *Growing Healthy Asian American Churches: Ministry Insights from Groundbreaking Congregations,* edited by Peter Cha et al., 201–08. Downers Grove, IL: InterVarsity, 2006.

Kaufman, Graham. *Shame: The Power of Caring.* Rochester, VT: Schenkman, 1992.

Keller, Timothy. *Center Church.* Grand Rapids, MI: Zondervan, 2012.

Kesler, Clive S. "Abdication of the Intellectuals: Sociology, Anthropology, and the Asian Values Debate—or, What Everybody Needed to Know about 'Asian Values' That Social Scientists Failed to Point Out." *Sojourn: Journal of Social Issues in Southeast Asia* 4 (1999) 295–312.

Kim, Dongsoo. "The Healing of *Han* in Korean Pentecostalism." *Journal of Pentecostal Theology* 15 (1999) 123–39.

Kim, Joo Yup, and Sang Hung Nam. "The Concept and Dynamics of Face: Implications for Organizational Behavior in Asia." *Organization Science* 9 (1998) 522–34.

Kim, Ki-hong. "Expression of Emotions by Americans and Koreans." *Korean Studies* 9 (1985) 38–56.

Kim, Kua-Ok. "What is Behind 'Face-Saving' in Cross-Cultural Communication?" *Intercultural Communication Studies* III (1993) 1–10.

Kim, Sharon. *A Faith of Our Own.* New Brunswick, NJ: Rutgers University Press, 2010.

Kim, Young-Joo. "Subject/Object Drop in the Acquisition of Korean: A Cross-Linguistic Comparison." First Language Acquisition of East Asian Languages. *Journal of East Asian Linguistics* 9 (October 2000) 325–51.

Kiss, Katalin É. "The Notion of Topic and Focus." *Angol Filológiai Tanulmányok. Hungarian Studies in English* (1977) 11, 211–23.

Kishimoto, Hideo. "Some Japanese cultural traits and religions." In *The Japanese Mind: Essentials of Japanese Philosophy and Culture,* edited by Charles Moore. Honolulu, HI: University of Hawaii Press (1967) 110–21.

Kohn, Lydia. *Introducing Daoism.* UK: Routledge, 2008.

Krishan, Yuvraj. "Karma Vipaka." *Numen.* Vol. XXX (1983) 199–214.

Kwon, Soo-Young. "Codependence and Interdependence: Cross-cultural Reappraisal of Boundaries and Relationality." *Pastoral Psychology* 50 (2001) 39–52.

Lai, Karyn L. "Confucian Moral Thinking." *Philosophy East & West* 45 (Apr 1995) 249–72.

Lan, Fung Yu. *A History of Chinese Philosophy, Volume I: The Period of the Philosophers.* Translated by Derk Bodde. Princeton, NJ: Princeton University Press, 1953.

Lee, Helen. "Healthy Leaders, Healthy Households 1." In *Growing Healthy Asian American Churches: Ministry Insights from Groundbreaking Congregations.* Edited by Peter Cha, et al., 51–76. Downers Grove, IL: InterVarsity, 2006.

———. "Silent Exodus: Can the East Asian Church in America Reverse the Flight of its Next Generation." *Christianity Today* 40(9) (1996) 50–54.

———. "Silent No More." *Christianity Today* 58(8) (2014) 38–47.

Li, Charles N. *Subject and Topic*. Waltham, MA: Academic, 1976.

Li, Chenyang. "The Confucian Concept of Jen and the Feminist Ethics of Care: A Comparative Study." *Hypatia* 9 (1994) 70–89.

———. "Shifting Perspectives: Filial Morality Revisited." *Philosophy East and West* 47:2 (Aug 1997) 211–32.

———. *The Tao Encounters the West: Explorations in Comparative Philosophy*. Albany, NY: SUNY Press, 1999.

Li, Chi, cited in Kwang-Kuo Hwang. "Chinese Relationalism: Theoretical Construction and Methodological Considerations." *Journal for the Theory of Social Behaviour* 30 (2000) 155–78.

Li-Hsiang, Lisa Rosenlee. *Confucianism and Women: A Philosophical Interpretation*. Albany, NY: SUNY Press, 2006.

Lin, Tung-chi. "The Chinese Mind: Its Taoist Substratum." *Journal of the History of Ideas* 8 (1947) 259–72.

Lin, Yutang. "Growing Old Gracefully." In *The Importance of Living*, 190–99. New York: Quill, 1937.

Ling, Samuel. *The "Chinese" Way of Doing Things*. Phillipsburg, NJ: Puritan and Reformed, 2004.

Littlejohn, Ronnie. *An Introduction to Daoism*. NY, NY: I.B. Tauris (I.B. Tauris Introductions to Religion), 2009.

Liu, Shu King. "The Origin of Taoism." *The Monist* 27 (1917) 376–89.

Lu, Aito, et al. "Looking up to Others: Social Status, Chinese Honorifics and Spatial Attention." *Canadian Journal of Experimental Psychology* 68 (2014) 77–83.

Marcella, Anthony J., et al. "Introduction: Approaches to Culture and Self." *Culture and Self,* edited by Anthony J. Marsella et al., 2–23. New York: Tavistock, 1985.

Markus, Hazel Rose, and Shinobu Kitayama. "Culture and the Self: Implications for Cognition, Emotion, and Motivation." *Psychological Review* 98 (1991) 224–53.

Matsumoto, Yoshiko, and Shigeko Okamoto. "The Construction of the Japanese Language and Culture in Teaching Japanese as a Foreign Language." *Japanese Language and Literature* 37 (April 2003) 27–48.

Maynard, K. Senko. "Grammar with an Attitude: on the Expressivity of Certain *da* Sentences in Japanese." *Linguistics* 37 (1999) 215–50.

Mencius, 179 4A:2.

Mitchell, Charles. *Short Example of International Business Culture*. Petaluma, CA: World Trade, 1999.

Mizutani, Osamu, and Nobuko Mizutani. "How to Be Polite in Japanese." Tokyo: Japan Times (1987) 117–18.

Moore, Charles R., ed. *The Chinese Mind: Essential of Chinese Philosophy and Culture*. Honolulu: HI; University of Hawaii Press, 1967.

Moxnes, Halvor. "Honor, Shame, and the Outside World in Paul's Letter to the Romans." *The Social World of Formative Christianity and Judaism: Essays in Tribute to Charles Clarke Kee,* edited by Jacob Neusner et al., 207–18. Philadelphia, PA: Fortress, 1988.

Naylor, Larry L. *American Culture: Myth and Reality of a Culture of Diversity*. Westport, CN: Praeger, 1998.

Nesbitt, Richard E. *The Geography of Thought: How Asians and Westerners Think Differently . . . and Why*. NY, New York: Free, 2003.

O'Dwyer, Shaun. "Democracy and Confucian Values." *Philosophy East and West* 53 (Jan 2003) 39–63.

Oetzel, John G., et al. "An Analysis of the Relationships among Face Concerns and Facework Behaviors in Perceived Conflict Situations: A Four-Culture Investigation." *International Journal of Conflict Management* 19 (2008) 382–403.

———. "A Typology of Facework Behaviors with Best Friends and Relative Strangers." *Communication Strategy* 48 (2000) 397–419.

Oh, Whachul. "Transforming Han: A Correlational Method for Psychology and Religion." *Journal of Religious Health* 54 (2015) 1099–1109.

Pak, Su Yon, et al. *Singing the Lord's Song in a New Land: Korean American Practices of Faith.* Louisville, KY: Westminster John Knox, 2005.

Palmer, Martha, and Zhibiao Wu. "Verb Semantics for English-Chinese Translation." *Machine Translation* 10 (1995) 59–92.

Park, Andrew Sung Park. *The Wounded Heart of God: The Asian Concept of Han and the Christian Doctrine of Sin.* Nashville, TN: Abingdon, 1993.

Park, M. Sydney, et al. *Honoring the Generations: Learning with Asian North American Congregations.* Valley Forge, PA: Judson, 2012.

Persons, Larry Scott. *Face Dynamics, Social Power, and Virtue Among Thai Leaders.* PhD diss., Fuller School of World Mission, 2008.

Piper, John. *Future Grace.* Sisters, OR: Multnomah, 1995.

Plantinga, Cornelius Jr. *Not the Way It's Supposed to Be: A Breviary of Sin.* Grand Rapids, MI: Eerdmans, 1999.

Poškaitė, Loreta. "The Treatment of Human Body in Chinese Traditional Culture." In *Eastwards: Western View on East Asian Culture,* edited by Frank Kranshaar, 257–72. NY, NY: Peter Lang International, 2010.

Qingzhong, Yang. "On the Dao on the Commentary of the Book of Change." *Frontiers of Philosophy in China* 1 (2006) 572–93.

Robertson, Christopher J. *The Global Dispersion of Chinese Values: A Three-Country Study of Confucian Dynamism. Management International Review* 40:3 (2000 3rd Quarter) 266.

Rösch, Martin, and Kay G. Segler. "Communication with Japanese." *Management International Review,* 27 (1987) 56–67.

Sande, Ken. *The Peacemaker: A Biblical Guide to Resolving Personal Conflict,* 3rd ed. Grand Rapids, MI: Baker, 2004.

Sangalang, Grace. *The Wall of Shame: How Shame Affects Relationships With God and Others in the Asian American Community.* MA thesis, Talbot School of Theology, 2013.

Saucy, Robert. *The Church in God's Program.* Chicago, IL: Moody, 1972.

———. "Theology of Human Nature." In *Christian Perspectives on Being Human: A Multidisciplinary Approach to Integration,* edited by James Porter and David. M. Ciocchi, 17–54. Grand Rapids, MI: Baker, 1993.

Schmitt, Bernd, et al. "Language and Consumer Memory: Impact of Linguistic Differences between Chinese and English." *Journal of Consumer Research* 21 (Dec 1994) 419–31.

Scofield, C. I. *Scofield Reference Notes to the Bible: 1917 Notes.* Oxford, UK: Oxford University Press, 1917.

"self." http://dictionary.reference.com/browse/self.

Shi, Dinxu. "Topic and Topic Comment Constructions in Mandarin Chinese." *Language* 76 (2000) 382–408.

Silzer, Sheryl Takagi. *Biblical Multicultural Teams: Applying Biblical Truth to Cultural Differences.* Pasadena, CA: William Carey International University Press, 2011.

————. "Confessions of a Confucianist." *Priscilla Papers* 23 (2009) 5–12.

————. "How Buddhist Spirituality Influences and Shapes Asian Cultural Practices: Missiological Implications." In *Seeking the Unseen: Spiritual Realities in the Buddhist World*, edited by Paul H. De Neui, 101–21. Pasadena, CA: William Carey Library, 2016.

Smedes, Lewis B. *Shame and Grace: Healing the Shame We Don't Deserve.* San Francisco, CA: Zondervan, 1993.

Smith, Donald I., et al. *The Gift of the Stranger. Faith, Hospitality, and Foreign Language Learning.* Grand Rapids, MI: Eerdmans, 2000.

Sohn, Ho-min. "The State of the Art in the Historical-Comparative Studies of Japanese and Korean." *Korean Studies* 4 (1980) 29–50.

Stewart, Edward C., and Milton J. Bennett. *American Cultural Patterns: A Cross Cultural Perspective.* Yarmouth, ME: Intercultural, 2005.

Stockitt, Robin. *Restoring the Shamed: Towards a Theology of Shame.* Eugene, OR: Cascade, 2012.

Sugikawa, Nancy, and Steve Wong. "Grace-Filled Households." In *Growing Healthy Asian American Churches: Ministry Insights from Groundbreaking Congregations,* edited by Peter Cha, et al., 19–38. Downers Grove, IL: InterVarsity, 2006.

Sung, Kyu-taik. "Elder Respect Exploration of Ideals and Forms in East Asia." *Journal of Aging Studies* 15 (Mar 2001) 13–26.

Sure, Rev. Heng. "Filial Respect and Buddhist Meditation." *Religion East and West* 1 (June 2001) 57–65.

Swartley, William M. "The Relation of Justice/Righteousness to Shalom/Eirene." *Ex Auditu* 22 (2006) 29–53.

Ten Elshoff, Gregg A. *Confucius for Christians: What an Ancient Chinese Worldview Can Teach Us about Life in Christ.* Grand Rapids, MI: Eerdmans, 2015.

Ting-Toomey, Stella. "Face and Facework: An Introduction." In *The Challenge of Facework: Cross-Cultural and Interpersonal Issues,* 1–14. Albany, NY: SUNY Press, 1994.

Tokunaga, Paul. *Invitation to Lead.* Downers Grove, IL: InterVarsity, 2003.

Toyama-Szeto, Nikki A. "Perfectionistic Tendencies." In *More Than Serving Tea: Asian American Women on Expectations, Relationships, Leadership and Faith,* edited by Nikki A. Toyama-Szeto and Tracey Gee, 50–68. Downers Grove, IL: InterVarsity, 2006.

Triandis, Harry C. "Individualism-Collectivism and Personality." *Journal of Personality* 69 (2001) 907–23.

Tseng, Wen-Shing, et al. *Asian Culture and Psychotherapy: Implications for East and West.* Honolulu, HI: University of Hawaii Press, 2005.

Turner, David L. "Paul and the Ministry of Reconciliation in 2 Corinthians 5:11; 6:2." *Criswell Theological Review* 4 (1989) 77–95.

Verhoeven, Martin. "Buddhist Ideas about No-self and the Person." *Religion East and West* 10 (2010) 93–112.

Walsh, Michael J. "The Economics of Salvation: toward a Theory of Exchange in Chinese Buddhism." *Journal of the American Academy of Religion* 75 (2007) 353–82.

Waltner, Erland. "Shalom and Wholeness." *Brethren Life and Thought* XXIX (1984) 145–51.

Wang, Robin R. *Yinyang: The Way of Heaven and Earth in Chinese Thought and Culture (New Approaches to Asian History).* Cambridge, England: Cambridge University Press, 2015.

Weiming, Tu. "The Ecological Turn in New Confucian Humanism." *Daedalus* (2001) 243–64.

———. "*Li* as Process of Humanization." In *Humanity and Self-Cultivation: Essays in Confucian Thought,* 17–34. Berkeley: Asian Humanities, 1979.

———. "Selfhood and Otherness in Confucian Thought." In *Culture and Self: Asian and Western Perspectives,* edited by Anthony J. Marsella, et al., 231–51. London: Tavistock, 1986.

White, Hugh C. *Shalom in the Old Testament.* Berea, OH: United Church, 1973.

Wierzbicka, Anna. "Emotion and Culture: Arguing with Martha Nussbaum." *Ethos* 31 (2003) 577–600.

———. "Japanese Key Words and Core Cultural Values." *Language in Society* 20 (1991) 333–85.

Wildavsky, Aaron. *The Nursing Father: Moses as a Political Leader.* Tuscaloosa, AL: University of Alabama Press, 1984.

Wilkins, Steve, and Mark L. Sanford. *Hidden Worldviews: Eight Cultural Stories that Shape Our Lives.* Downers Grove, IL: InterVarsity, 2009.

Willard, Dallas. *Renovation of the Heart: Putting on the Character of Christ.* Colorado Springs, CO: NavPress, 2012.

Wolf, Arthur, ed. *Religion and Ritual in Chinese Society.* Stanford, CA: Stanford University Press, 1974.

Wong, Hoover. *Coming Together or Coming Apart?* Pasadena, CA: TRACC, 1998.

Wu, Jackson. "Grace, Gift-giving, Guanxi in Chinese Culture." Jackson Wu: Doing Theology, Thinking Mission, February 17, 2016, accessed February 17, 2016.

———. "Saved by Grace? Which Kind?" Jackson Wu: Doing Theology, Thinking Mission, January 20, 2016, accessed January 20, 2016.

———. *Saving God's Face: A Chinese Contextualization of Salvation through Honor and Shame.* Pasadena, CA: William Carey International University, 2012.

Yang, Fenggang. *Chinese Christians in America: Conversion, Assimilation, and Adhesive Identities.* University Park, PA: Pennsylvania State University Press, 1999.

Yang, Suying. "The Parameter of Temporal Endpoint and the Basic Function of *–le. Journal of East Asian Linguisics* 20 (Nov 2011) 383–415.

Yao, Xinzhong. "Confucius, the Founder of Confucianism." *Dialogue and Alliance* 12 (1998) 20–33.

Yasuda, Sachiko. "Learning Phrasal Verbs Through Conceptual Metaphors." *TESOL Quarterly* 44 (2010) 250–73.

Yep, Jeannette, et al. *Following Jesus Without Dishonoring Your Parents.* Downers Grove, IL: InterVarsity, 1998.

Yim, Dawnhee. "Psychocultural Features of Ancestor Worship in Modern Korean Society." In *Confucianism and the Family,* edited by Walter H. Slote and George A. DeVos, 163–87. Albany, NY: SUNY Press (1998).

Yoo, David K., and Ruth H. Chung. *Religion and Spirituality in Korean America.* Urbana IL: University of Illinois Press, 2008.

Yu, Ning. "What Does our Face Mean to us?" In *From Body to Meaning in Culture: Papers on Semantic Cognitive Studies of Chinese,* 151–86. Amsterdam, Netherlands: John Benjamins, 2009.

Zhang, Helen, and Geoff Baker. *Inside the Chinese Mind: A Guide on How the Chinese Think.* Singapore: Cengage Learning Asia, 2012.

Index